COLLECTED WISDOM FOR THE JOURNEY

Along the Road to Manhood

STU WEBER

FAMILY
CHRISTIAN
PRESS

ALONG THE ROAD TO MANHOOD
Published by Multnomah Publishers, Inc.

©1995 by Stu Weber
International Standard Book Number: 0-88070-845-X
Special FCP Edition: 1-893065-25-1

Cover illustration by Martin French
Cover designed by BigPicture Design

Printed in the United States of America

Most Scripture quotations are from: New American Standard Bible (NASB)
©1960, 1977 by the Lockman Foundation.

Also quoted: The Holy Bible, New International Version (NIV) ©1973, 1984 by
International Bible Society, used by permission of Zondervan Publishing House

The King James Version (KJV)

The Living Bible (TLB) ©1971 by Tyndale House Publishers

The New Testament in Modern English, Revised Edition (Phillips) ©1972 by
J.B. Phillips

The New English Bible (NEB) ©1961, 1970 by Cambridge University Press

FOR INFORMATION:
MULTNOMAH PUBLISHERS, INC.
POST OFFICE BOX 1720
SISTERS, OREGON 97759

99 00 01 02 03 04 — 7 6 5 4 3 2 1

TO ERIC WEBER

my brother by birth, in spirit, for life

"Let us run with endurance
the race that is set before us, fixing our eyes on Jesus,
the author and perfecter of faith…consider Him,
so that you may not grow weary and lose heart."

HEBREWS 12:1-3

Last spring I visited my son in England, where he is pursuing graduate studies. Late one afternoon I found myself wandering along the cobblestones of Broad Street in Oxford.

There, imbedded in countless dark gray stones forming the road's surface, were twenty-four white stones. They stood out not only for their color, but for their pattern as well. They formed a simple cross on this thoroughfare of the western world's most prestigious university city.

As the bustling traffic surged by—heedless of crosses and white stones—my mind sought to push back the years to the scene memorialized by the marker.

Such simple stones. Such an enormous event. Such profound instruction.

It was a crisp October day in 1555, a day that dawned like a thousand October mornings before, but a day destined to stand out among the thousands. Two men, refusing to recant their personal faith in Jesus Christ, would die a terrible death that morning. They would be burned at the stake.

What crossed their minds, that fine autumn day, as these two men walked through the doors of dreary Bocardo Prison and into the sunlight of their last moments on earth? We can't know all that was in their thoughts; yet we have more than stones in the pavement to mark their passing.

We have a few of their words, as well.

We know that as they approached the stake, Hugh Latimer turned to Nicholas Ridley and said,

"Be of good cheer, Ridley. Play the man. We shall this day light such a candle, by God's grace,...as I trust shall never be put out."

"Play the man!" Three words; one point. Sound advice.

As needed today as it was in 1555. Whether to lift one man's soul in a moment of crisis, or to lift an entire gender's soul in a culture of crisis.

Play the man. Be all God intended you to be. Stay strong. Stay pure. Stay faithful. Play the man.

I mused on Latimer's words as the afternoon Oxford traffic flowed by...and the words drew me close to the hearts of these two men. Words are like markers, aren't they? Like white cobblestones on a busy thoroughfare, they mark a man's passage. We see something of his journey into manhood, and in seeing, we better our own course.

The world's traffic rushes by, just as it always has, but for a moment in time...you find yourself locking arms with one who has walked the long road before you.

The quotes contained in this little book are like that. Don't think of them as words, but as markers on the journey. As milestones of a man's life, they merit careful thought. It might mean stepping out of the traffic for a moment or two—pulling off life's busy highway and doing a little pondering. Read one or two of these thoughts at a sitting. Then sit. Take them, like a good steak, one bite at a time. Taste. Savor. Chew on them. Turn them over in your mind. And then, as Latimer told Ridley, *play the man.*

But what does it mean to play the man? Where do you and I go to look for true masculinity? Voices shout confusing and contradictory directions from the roadside. Signs point every which way. Would-be models lead off onto dangerous sideroads and destructive dead-ends. How is a man to find his way? Where is the true road? I suggest what should already be obvious.

The true road to manhood is a Man Himself. Jesus Christ is the ultimate Man. Maximum manhood. The perfect Model. The complete Hero. The Way, the Truth, and the Life. In Him, we see all four pillars of manhood: King, Warrior,

Mentor, and Friend. He made the long journey from heaven to leave footprints on earth...footprints that a man can follow. As Scripture tells us, "Let us run with endurance the race that is set before us, fixing our eyes on Jesus, the author and perfecter of faith...consider Him, so that you may not grow weary and lose heart" (Hebrews 12:1-3).

He came as the King. He saw us in our need, looked into our dark and hopeless future and saw that apart from His help we had no help. In His great love for us, He provided for our needs and paid all our debts, even to the point of laying down His own life.

He came as a Warrior. As David squared off against the enemy of his people in the Valley of Elah, so the Son of David stood alone against death and hell and the Great Dragon on a hill called Golgotha. He saw the need, and He took appropriate action—at the cost of His own blood.

He came as Mentor. They called Him "Rabbi" and

"Teacher." With patience and skill He taught eternal truths on the hillsides, out on the lake, and along the winding, dusty pathways. Wisdom was on His tongue, and He drew unforgettable lessons from common objects in every day life…farmers and seed, birds and fish, flowers and fields, soldiers and housewives, storm clouds and city lights.

He came as Friend. He sought out men and women. He called little children into His arms. He befriended the rejected and friendless. He shared His life plans and dreams, enjoyed intimate dinner parties, festive occasions, and the warmth of a comradely campfire. Ultimately, He laid down His very life for the sake of His friends.

King, Warrior, Mentor, and Friend. He displayed all four of these traits on His journey through manhood, and if we would be His men, so must we.

As Joe Stowell writes: "Jesus Christ does not at all diminish our manhood. He emerges through the distinct qualities of maleness to create a fuller and richer expression of what a man can be. He redefines our manhood by replacing the motivations of our world with new guidelines for success. He directs our manhood along the path of ultimate significance. He takes our instincts to protect, provide, conquer, and accumulate, and points them in productive directions."[1]

So go for it, man! Keep your eyes on Him, and step out on that masculine journey with clear eyes and a firm stride. But don't forget to read the roadside markers along the way. Don't forget to ponder the counsel of those who have walked before you and walk alongside you. It's a good way to stay on the right road. And that's what this little book is all about.

1. Joseph M. Stowell, "The Making of a Man," *Moody Monthly*, May 1992, p. 4.

THE KING

(PROVIDER)

"Whoever wishes to become
great among you shall be your servant,
and whoever wishes to be first among you shall
be your slave; just as the Son of Man did not
come to be served, but to serve."

MATTHEW 20:26-28

When we speak of the King as one of the four pillars of masculinity, we are talking of King Jesus, not King Tut. No thrones, harems, palm branches, and peeled grapes here.

The King Himself said it best: "Whoever wishes to become great among you shall be your servant, and whoever wishes to be first among you shall be your slave; just as the Son of Man did not come to be served, but to serve" (Matthew 20:26-28).

The heart of the king is a provisionary heart, and the key element in "provision" is *vision*. Pro-vision means "vision before hand." The king in a man looks ahead, scans the horizon, anticipates needs, spots potential dangers, defines direction, and charts a wise course. Out of the king flows a sense of purpose, stability, and justice. When the king is home the castle is secure. When Dad is functioning, everyone enjoys stability.

When the king function is out of balance in a man, everything is shaky. People tremble. Relationships totter. Finances crumble. And the home feels more like a hospital ward than a castle.

A true king is neither a tyrant nor a passive "victim of circumstances." Perhaps the only thing worse than a dictator is a leader who refuses to lead at all. A king is not passive. When the king fails, the kingdom falls. When the king is absent or abusive, the family experiences dysfunction. The climate becomes oppressive. Disorder and chaos rule.

But when Dad is dad, there is peace, prosperity, justice, and love. As another described it, home is but an earlier heaven. What confidence this kind of leadership brings—to an organization, to a church, to a family! A provisionary king keeps the larger issues before his family or organization so they won't be overcome by temporary setbacks or the disorienting fog of daily circumstances. Clarity of vision is critical to health.

And the king lives with his eyes on the horizon. In the quiet moments of his day, he asks himself questions such as these:

If our marriage were to go on just the way it's been going, what will it be like for us in five, ten, or twenty years?

How can I help my eight-year-old daughter learn to understand and control her emotions before the hormones start pumping through her body?

When will my young son and I need to have our first talk about sex?

What kinds of things might my kids encounter in middle school—and how can I prepare them?

How can I manage my career goals so that I'm available to my high school children?

What will my children need in a dad when they're in college?

What kind of traits will my grandkids cherish in their grandfather?

What kind of legacy do I long to leave the generations who will follow in our family?

These are some of the questions that rise in the heart of the king.

"There was a man in the land of Uz, whose name was Job, and that man was blameless, upright, fearing God, and turning away from evil. And seven sons and three daughters were born to him. His possessions also were 7,000 sheep, 3,000 camels, 500 yoke of oxen, 500 female donkeys, and very many servants; and that man was the greatest of all the men of the east.... [Job made a habit of] rising early in the morning and offering burnt offerings according to the number...[of his children]; for Job said, 'Perhaps my sons have sinned and cursed God in their hearts.' Thus Job did continually."

—JOB 1:1-5

"An almost perfect relationship with his father was the earthly root of all his wisdom. From his own father, he said, he learned that Fatherhood must be at the core of the universe. He was thus prepared in an unusual way to teach that religion in which the relation of the Father and Son is of all relationships the most central."

—C.S. LEWIS

Writing of George MacDonald, *George Mac Donald: An Anthology*

"Far beyond what you would expect, far beyond what logic would dictate, men seek to know their fathers."

— BRIAN NEWMAN
From *The Father Book*

"I tell you the truth, the Son can do nothing by himself; he can do only what he sees his Father doing, because whatever the Father does the Son also does. For the Father loves the Son and shows him all he does."

— JESUS (JOHN 5:19-20, NIV)

Across the fields of yesterday
He sometimes comes to me
A little lad just back from play
The boy I used to be.
He smiles at me so wistfully
When once he's crept within
It is as though he had hoped to see
The man I might have been.

— AUTHOR UNKNOWN

"C'mon, dads.... Let's start saying no to more and more of the things that pull us farther and farther away from the ones who need us the most.... You're not perfect? So, what else is new? You don't know exactly how to pull it off? Welcome to the club!... Your family doesn't expect profound perfection, command performances, or a superhuman plan. Just you—warts and all.... Let's get started."

—CHARLES R. SWINDOLL
From *The Strong Family*

"The highest reward for a man's toil is not what he gets for it, but what he becomes by it."

—JOHN RUSKIN

"And he will restore the hearts of the fathers to their children, and the hearts of the children to their fathers, lest I come and smite the land with a curse."

—MALACHI 4:6

"Do not hinder [the children] from coming to Me; for the kingdom of heaven belongs to such as these."

—JESUS (MATTHEW 19:14)

"Power is of two kinds. One is obtained by the fear of punishment and the other by the art of love. Power based on love is a thousand times more effective and permanent than the one derived by the fear of punishment."

—MOHANDAS GANDHI
As quoted in *Husbands Who Won't Lead and Wives Who Won't Follow*,
by James Walker

Seven Watchmen sitting in a tower,
Watching what had come upon mankind,
Showed the man the glory and the power,
And bade him shape the kingdom of his mind.

—RUDYARD KIPLING
As quoted in *Husbands Who Won't Lead and Wives Who Won't Follow*,
by James Walker

"In many cases dad thinks he is the head of the house and mom may even let him believe it. But in reality she manages everything. Most of the time he doesn't even know what's going on.... She decides what the children can or cannot do. She checks on their schoolwork, talks to their teachers, and signs their report cards. She helps them work out their problems, teaches them what they need to know, and takes them where they need to be.... Studies have shown that there is a direct correlation between a weak father figure and a child's problems in areas such as character, conduct, and achievement."

—RICHARD STRAUSS
From *Confident Children and How They Grow*

"A dad is the person who can turn a seeming calamity into a smile by turning the light side up."

—ROGER L. KERR
From *The Family Album*

THE HEADSHIP OF THE CHRISTIAN HUSBAND

"Christian law has crowned him in the permanent relationship of marriage, bestowing—or should I say, inflicting?—a certain 'headship' on him.... The husband is the head of the wife just in so far as he is to her what Christ is to the Church. He is to love her as Christ loved the Church—read on—and gave his life for her (Ephesians 5:25). This headship, then, is most fully embodied not in the husband we should all wish to be but in him whose marriage is most like a crucifixion; whose wife receives most and gives least, is most unworthy of him, is—in her own mere nature—least lovable. For the Church has no beauty but what the Bridegroom gives her; he does not find, but makes her, lovely. The chrism of this terrible coronation is to be seen not in the joys of any man's marriage but in its sorrows, in the sickness and sufferings of a good wife or the faults of a bad one; in his unwearying (never paraded) care of his inexhaustible forgiveness; forgiveness, not acquiescence. As Christ sees in the flawed, proud, fanatical, or lukewarm Church on earth that Bride who will one day be without spot or wrinkle, and labours to produce the latter, so the husband whose headship is Christ-like (and he is allowed no other sort) never despairs....

"The sternest feminist need not grudge my sex the crown offered to it either in the Pagan or the Christian mystery. For the one is of paper and the other of thorns. The real danger is not that husbands may grasp the latter too eagerly; but that they will allow or compel their wives to usurp it."

—C.S. LEWIS
From *The Four Loves*

"There is a special father-pride in raising a son because the dad identifies. You love to see him do what you did; even more, to see him do what you never did or couldn't do."

—RAY ORTLUND
From *A Man and His Loves*

"It is easier to build a boy than to mend a man."

—AUTHOR UNKNOWN
From Croft M. Pentz's *The Complete Book of Zingers*

"No matter how hard I tried to put myself back into my kids' lives, it didn't work. They had adjusted to the point where having Dad around wasn't necessary. Now, seven years later, we're a little happier, but it's not anything like I wish it could be. I missed my chance, and *now it's too late*. [Those are] four words you never want to say."

—GREG JOHNSON AND MIKE YORKEY
From "Daddy's Home" in *Raising Them Right*

"Studies show that the absence of the father expresses itself in male children in two very different ways: it is linked to increased aggressiveness on one hand, and greater manifestations of effeminacy on the other."

—JAMES DOBSON AND GARY BAUER,
From *Children at Risk*

"Whoever causes one of these little ones who believe in me to stumble, it is better for him that a heavy millstone be hung around his neck, and that he be drowned in the depth of the sea."

—JESUS (MATTHEW 18:6)

"From time to time I have felt for my father a longing that is almost physical, something passionate, but prior to sex—something infantile, profound. It has bewildered me.… It is mysterious to me exactly what it is I wanted from my father. I have seen this longing in other men—and see it now in my own sons, their longing for me.… Perhaps it is some urge of Telemachus, the residual infant in the man still wistful for the father's heroic protection. One seeks to return not to the womb…but to a different thing, a father's sponsorship in the world. A boy wants the aura and the armament of his father."

—LANCE MORROW
From *The Chief, a Memoir of Fathers and Sons*

"You have just finished a run, and you are sitting on the porch sweating like a horse and smelling like one, and your son, or perhaps a little neighbor boy, sits down next to you, leans against you, and says, 'You smell good.' This is the primal longing for one's father."

—KENT HUGHES
From *Disciplines of a Godly Man*

"...I have chosen him, in order that he may command his children and his household after him to keep the way of the Lord by doing righteousness and justice."

—GENESIS 18:19

"...Take now your son, your only son, whom you love...and go to the land of Moriah; and offer him there as a burnt offering on one of the mountains of which I will tell you.... *So the two of them walked on together....* 'God will provide for Himself the lamb for the burnt offering, my son.' *So the two of them walked on together.*"

—GENESIS 22:2, 6, 8

"Forty percent of children go to sleep without their fathers and forty percent of them have not seen their father for a year.... The trend toward father absence has reached a crisis. It is a national crisis—not one of many crises, but the national crisis of our time."

—DR. WADE HORN
From a Dallas newspaper report

Papa's gonna' make it all right
So Hushabye, don't you cry
You're gonna flourish and you're gonna grow
Like daffodils on golden hills
Papa's gonna scare off the storms—
No rain will fall on your head.
Papa's gonna make it all right!

—FROM THE MUSICAL, *SHENANDOAH*

"Labor to keep alive in your breast that little spark of celestial fire called conscience."

—GEORGE WASHINGTON
From "Rules of Civility"

"A dad is the person who always knows that time is a great leveler. He has the patience, born of experience, that takes the long view and sees the sun shining beyond the present storm."

—ROGER L. KERR
From *The Family Album*

"Life's greatest joys are not what one does apart from the work of one's life, but with the work of one's life. Those who have missed the joy of work, of a job well done, have missed something very important. This applies to our children, too. When we want our children to be happy, we want them to enjoy life. We want them to find and enjoy their work in the world."

—WILLIAM J. BENNETT
From *The Book of Virtues*

"Excellence in childrearing does not evolve from making fewer mistakes than everybody else. It evolves from making plenty of mistakes and learning from them."

—DR. RAY GUARENDI
From *Back to the Family*

"Fathering makes a man, whatever his standing in the eyes of the world, feel strong and good and important, just as he makes his child feel loved and valued.... Fathering is the most masculine thing a man can do."

—FRANK S. PITTMAN III
From *Man Enough*

ONLY A DAD

Only a dad with a brood of four,
One of ten million men or more
Plodding along in the daily strife,
Bearing the whips and the scorns of life,
With never a whimper of pain or hate,
For the sake of those who at home await.

Only a dad, neither rich nor proud,
Merely one of the surging crowd,
Toiling, striving from day to day,
Facing whatever may come his way,
Silent whenever the harsh condemn,
And bearing it all for the love of them.

Only a dad but he gives his all,
To smooth the way for his children small,
Doing with courage stern and grim
The deeds that his father did for him.
This is the line that for him I pen:
Only a dad, but the best of men.

— EDGAR GUEST

"A word here, a glance there, a time together, a time apart—which will be the moments that will rise up in memory and shape the child that looks without judgment on all that you do and say?"

—KENT NEWBORN
From *Letters to My Son*

"Lord, every path I walked with Dad, has led to You."

—RUTH HARMS CALKIN
From *Lord, You Love to Say Yes*

"Sometimes, when my husband shares his big leather lounge chair with one of his children during a basketball game or the evening news, I can see that they see him as a bulwark, an authority, a sort of deity. And a big kid. The kind of father who is strong enough to inform, secure enough to say, "I don't know," warm enough to kiss and cuddle, and wild enough to invent the knuckle machine (tickling game)."

—ANNE QUINDLEN
From *The Making of a Father*

"No man can possibly know what life means, what the world means, until he has a child and loves it. And then the whole universe changes and nothing will ever again seem exactly as it seemed before."

—LAFCADIO HEARN
19th century American writer

"It is not flesh and blood, but the heart which makes us fathers and sons."

—JOHANN VON SCHILLER
From *To Be a Father*

"Children's children are the crown of old men, and the glory of children is their father."

—PROVERBS 17:6 (KJV)

"My dad is my hero. He takes me places and spends time with me. We were looking for a present for my uncle in Massachusetts, and he pulled over so I could see a waterfall. It wasn't a big waterfall, but it was pretty."

—CHRIST VELEZ, EIGHT YEARS OLD
From *The Eugene Register Guard*

"A happy family is but an earlier heaven."

—SIR JOHN BROWNING

"I find too few words to adequately express my humble gratefulness to God for…the warm open affection, the generosity, the truly humble spirit, and the singleness of purpose I saw exemplified in daddy."

—GIGI (GRAHAM) TCHIVIDIJIAN
From *Thank You Lord for Home*

"Prayer guarantees that I am seeing my role as father for what it really is—a spiritual calling, the most important assignment God will ever give me."

—PAUL LEWIS
From "Secrets of a Winning Dad," *Charisma*

"If you take being a father seriously, you'll know that you're not big enough for the job, not by yourself…. Being a father will put you on your knees if nothing else ever did."

—ELISABETH ELLIOT
From *The Mark of a Man*

"What was it, this being 'a good father'? To love one's sons and daughters was not enough; to carry in one's bone and blood a pride in them, a longing for their growth and development—this was not enough. One had to be a ready companion to games and jokes and outings, to earn from the world this accolade."

—LAURA HOBSON
From *The First Papers*

"One thing I know: the only ones among you who will be really happy are those who will have sought and found how to serve."

—ALBERT SCHWEITZER

"Now comes a real heavy and it's strictly for dads…. No little child will think more of God than he thinks of his father."

—CHARLIE SHEDD
From *Smart Dads I Know*

"Fatherhood is a rite of passage of sorts. No matter how thoroughly you prepare for it, you're not prepared. You can't know what it's going to be like until you go through it."

—PAUL WARREN
From *The Father Book*

"I am thankful that being the head of the household doesn't mean I always must be in front. Dad doesn't have to be first in line to command attention and respect."

—KEL GROSECLOSE
From *Coming Up Short in a Tall World*

"Becoming a father is a spiritual event for the Christian man. He recognizes that fatherhood is a calling. It is a God-given vocation, not unlike being a missionary, preacher, or teacher."

—PAUL HEIDEBRECHT
From *Fathering a Son*

"Fatherhood is a remarkable undertaking, and unique adventure."

—ALVIN SCHWARTZ
From *To Be a Father*

"My wife and I are just exactly like many thousands of other families in America tonight. We have home our son, and what is far more important…our grand-children have home their daddy."

—FORMER PRESIDENT DWIGHT EISENHOWER
From Thanksgiving Day speech, 1953

"Everyday life must always be lived out against the back-drop of eternity…my job as a parent is a temporary responsibility with eternal consequences."

—TIM KIMMEL
From *Little House on the Freeway*

"Motherhood is woven throughout Scripture. But the ultimate responsibility of leadership in parenting is con-sistently laid at one place: At the feet of the father."

—MARY FARRAR
From *Choices*

"Father means looking at work and life in an entirely different manner. Suddenly a young husband is aware of the immense responsibility he is handed in protecting this family and furnishing food, shelter, clothing, tuition, braces, camps, for the next eighteen years. He can no longer easily say, 'Take this job and shove it,' or, 'Let's spend Christmas in Vail.' Along with these new responsibilities come fears—fear of taking second place in his wife's affections, fear of the baby's fragility, fear of not being a good father, and a very realistic fear that the couple's relationship will change."

—DOLORES CURRAN
From *Stress and the Healthy Family*

"Good fathering isn't exactly like good football, but the game demonstrates how important it is to pay attention to fundamentals if we hope to win. Here's to a long winning streak on your home turf!"

—AUTHOR UNKNOWN

"Manhood is composed of two sorts of men—those who love and create, and those who hate and destroy."

—JOSE MARTI
Letter to a Cuban farmer

"Authority does not make you a leader; it gives you the opportunity to be one."

—AUTHOR UNKNOWN
From Croft M. Pentz's *The Complete Book of Zingers*

"At the end, only two things really matter to a man, regardless of who he is, and they're the affection and understanding of his family. Anything and everything else he creates are insubstantial. They are ships given over to the mercy of the winds and the tides of prejudice, but the family is an everlasting anchorage, a quiet harbor where a man's ships can be left to swing to the moorings of pride and loyalty."

—ADMIRAL RICHARD BYRD
Written on his deathbed

"Try staying a few extra minutes at work, closing your office door, putting your feet up and closing your eyes for a while. Or, you can go for a short walk, maybe get a soda and read the newspaper. Draw some refreshment before you get home so you'll be free to interact with your children right away."

—THE NATIONAL CENTER FOR FATHERING

"Where a man belongs is up early and alone with God seeking vision and direction for his family."

—JOHN PIPER
From *Desiring God*

"If you don't know where you're going, you'll probably end up somewhere else."

—DAVID CAMPBELL

"Prayer is the exercise of the man who is a spiritual self-starter."

—STEVE FARRAR
From *Point Man*

"Ye are the light of the world. A city that is set on a hill cannot be hid. Neither do men light a candle, and put it under a bushel, but on a candlestick; and it giveth light unto all that are in the house. Let your light so shine before men, that they may see your good works, and glorify your Father which is in heaven."

—JESUS (MATTHEW 5:14-16, KJV)

"Pilgrims with no vision of the promised land become proprietors of their own land.... Instead of looking upward at [the Lord], they look inward at themselves and outward at each other. The result? Cabin fever. Quarreling families. Restless leaders. Fence building. Staked-off territory. No trespassing! signs are hung on hearts and homes. Spats turn into fights as myopic groups turn to glare at each other's weaknesses instead of turning to worship their common Strength."

—MAX LUCADO
From *God Came Near*

"He who spares the rod hates his son, but he who loves him is careful to discipline him."

—PROVERBS 13:24 (NIV)

"In the real world, we dads are called upon to father like football was originally played: Every man did his best at the game."

—PAUL LEWIS

fa'•ther: (NOUN) one who has begotten a child; a male parent, (VERB) to accept or claim responsibility for; to treat as a father, to care for

—DICTIONARY DEFINITION

"Home should be a retreat to which a son or daughter can return in triumph or defeat, in victory or disgrace, and know they will be loved."

—AUTHOR UNKNOWN

From Croft M. Pentz's *The Complete Book of Zingers*

"You pull into the driveway and turn off the engine. You lean over to collect your briefcase or lunch box and hard hat. As you sit up, you notice a little face peering through the window of your house. When you walk in the front door, your child is there to greet you and wrap his arms around your leg.

"It's nice to be welcomed back after eight to ten hours of absence, and those first few minutes can determine a great deal of what transpires in the remaining hours before bedtime."

—THE NATIONAL CENTER FOR FATHERING

"The disciplining of children is a vital part of child rearing and training. But it must always be in the context of love, self-control, and discretion. Parents must love their children enough to say 'no' and to correct them when needed. Firmness without love is harshness; love without firmness is softness. Love must be tender and tough."

—HENRY GARIEPY
From *Wisdom to Live By*

"Fatherlessness is now approaching parity with fatherhood as a defining feature of American childhood. Tonight, more than one-third of our nation's children will go to sleep in homes in which their fathers do not live. Before they reach age 18, more than half of our nation's children are likely to spend at least a significant portion of their childhood living apart from their fathers. Never before in our nation's history have so many children been voluntarily abandoned by their fathers."

— DAVID BLANKENHORN
From "The Other America—Fatherless Children"

"The family is not a liberal or a conservative idea, and it is not held together predominantly by government policies. Strong families, and particularly a strong commitment to fatherhood, is as much the work of culture."

— DON EBERLY
From "Revival of Fatherhood"

"Dad, I want to thank you for the loving discipline I received. The angry words of some of my friends' parents—"Son, this is going to hurt me more than it does you"—did not always ring true as I witnessed the cold application of punishment. Yes, I remember hearing you speak those words too, but you needn't have said them. Your moist eyes always stung more deeply than your hand."

—STEVE BARCLIFT
Quote taken from letter written to his father a few months before his father,
Joyce Barclift, died in a traffic accident.

"The LORD'S curse is on the house of the wicked, but he blesses the home of the righteous."

—PROVERBS 3:33 (NIV)

"When we first bend over the cradle of our own child, God throws back the temple door and reveals to us the sacredness and mystery of the father's and mother's love to ourselves."

—HENRY WARD BEECHER

"One of a father's primary responsibilities is to provide for his family's needs. When you are away at work, it doesn't mean you're no longer a father. If you remind yourself throughout the day that you are doing this for the ones you love, the transition back into the home won't be nearly as jarring."

—THE NATIONAL CENTER FOR FATHERING

"A good name is more desirable than great riches; to be esteemed is better than silver or gold."

—PROVERBS 22:1 (NIV)

"Dad is destiny. More than virtually any other factor, a biological father's presence in the family will determine a child's success and happiness. Rich or poor, white or black, the children of divorce and those born outside marriage struggle through life at a measurable disadvantage, according to a growing chorus of social thinkers."

—JOSEPH P. SHAPIRO AND JOANNIE M. SCHROF
Quoted in "Honor Thy Children," *U.S. News and World Report,*
February 27, 1995

"This is the final test of a gentleman: his respect for those who can be of no possible value to him."

—WILLIAM LYON PHELPS

"A real leader faces the music even when he doesn't like the tune."

—AUTHOR UNKNOWN

"Not the cry but the flight of the wild duck leads the flock to fly and follow."

—CHINESE PROVERB

"Leadership is the power to evoke the right response in other people."

—HUMPHREY MYNORS

"The healthy and strong individual is the one who asks for help when he needs it—whether he's got an abscess on his knee or in his soul."

—AUTHOR UNKNOWN

IF

If you can keep your head when all about you
Are losing theirs and blaming it on you;
If you can trust yourself when all men doubt you,
But make allowance for their doubting too;
If you can wait and not be tired by waiting,
Or, being lied about, don't deal in lies,
Or, being hated, don't give way to hating,
And yet don't look too good, nor talk too wise;
If you can dream—and not make dreams your master;
If you can think—and not make thoughts your aim;
If you can meet with triumph and disaster
And treat those two impostors just the same;
If you can bear to hear the truth you've spoken
Twisted by knaves to make a trap for fools,
Or watch the things you gave life to broken,
And stoop and build 'em up with worn-out tools;
If you can make one heap of all your winnings
And risk it on one turn of pitch-and-toss
And lose, and start again at your beginnings
And never breathe a word about your loss;

If you can force your heart and nerve and sinew
To serve your turn long after they are gone,
And so hold on when there is nothing in you
Except the Will which says to them: "Hold on!"
If you can talk with crowds and keep your virtue,
Or walk with kings—nor lose the common touch;
If neither foes nor loving friends can hurt you;
If all men count with you, but none too much;
If you can fill the unforgiving minute
With sixty seconds' worth of distance run—
Yours is the Earth and everything that's in it,
And—which is more—you'll be a Man, my son!

—RUDYARD KIPLING

"Those who love deeply never grow old; they may die of old age, but they die young."

—SIR ARTHUR WING PINERO

"Discipline your son, and he will give you peace; he will bring delight to your soul."

—PROVERBS 29:17 (NIV)

"I am an optimist. It doesn't seem too much use being anything else."

—WINSTON CHURCHILL

"See into life—don't just look at it."

—AUTHOR UNKNOWN

"To nourish children and raise them against odds is in any time, any place, more valuable than to fix bolts in cars or design nuclear weapons."

—AUTHOR UNKNOWN

"The true worth of a man is to be measured by the objects he pursues."

—MARCUS AURELIUS

"A man must first govern himself ere he is fit to govern a family; and his family ere he is fit to bear the government of the commonwealth."

—SIR WALTER RALEIGH

BLESS HIM, O LORD

Mender of toys, leader of boys,
Changer of fuses, kisser of bruises,
Bless him, dear Lord.
Hanger of screens, counselor of teens,
Fixer of bikes, chastiser of tykes,
Help him, O Lord.
Raker of leaves, cleaner of eaves,
Dryer of dishes, fulfiller of wishes,
Guard him, O Lord.

—AUTHOR UNKNOWN
From Roger L. Kerr's *The Family Album*

"...It's a long drive home for the new father in the small morning hours, and when he arrives, he is full of thought. His life has taken a permanent turn toward rectitude and sobriety and a decent regard for the sanctity of life; having seen his flesh in a layette, he wants to talk about some deep truths he has discovered in the past few hours to his own parents..."

—GARRISON KEILLOR
From *Lake Wobegon Days*

"It is a wonderful heritage to have an honest father."

—PROVERBS 20:7 (TLB)

"A father is a man who feels and shares and cries, who laughs and wrestles and hopes. He's a man who listens even when he doesn't understand. He's a man who loves even when he feels too weary. He stops doing what he thinks is important to do something else that may be even more important. A father is a man who is honest enough to realize that his responsibilities must determine his priorities."

—TIM HANSEL
From *What Kids Need Most in a Dad*

"A father is love. A father is someone who goes through a lot of pain and sorrow, but he is still a father. A father is not someone who runs away from life. He is there to cope and work things out. A father is love."

—MARY, A TEENAGE GIRL
From *What Kids Need Most in a Dad*

"A daughter, especially as she grows, is, to a father, a mystery, a fascination, a wonder. A son he can understand better, he's been there. But a daughter—! Oh, a daughter!"

—RAY ORTLUND
From *A Man and His Loves*

"Promise your family a stable home; you can start by giving them a stable dad."

—GARY SMALLEY AND JOHN TRENT
From *What Makes a Man?*

"Men, we don't need to follow our kids around pointing out every mistake or informing them of all their shortcomings. They need a family shepherd dedicated to building them up and encouraging them. One who believes in them and will bring out the best in them."

—DAVE SIMMONS
From *Father Power*

"Death is more universal than life; everyone dies but not everyone lives."

—ALAN SACHS

"A dad is the person who sets the example his children most want to emulate. His industry, devotion and care are the heritage his sons and daughters carry with them throughout their lives."

—ROGER L. KERR
From *The Family Album*

"…It was the light that shone in Daddy's eyes when we wore our frilly pink Easter dresses that made us glad to be little girls."

—HEATHER HARPHAM
From *Daddy, Where Were You?*

"Like Joseph, we are foster fathers and foster mothers, charged with caring for some of God's children while they live on earth and with preparing them for eternal life with their Father."

—BERT GHEZZI
From *Imitating St. Joseph*

"A good father is a bit of a mother."

—LEE SALK
From "Quotable Quotes," *Reader's Digest*, June 1978

"If a man's children are absolutely clear about how much he loves them, accepts them, admires them and wants to see them thrive in the world, they can face the world with special confidence."

—DAVID NICHOLS
From *Fathers Are Not Mothers*

"I mean, what have I done in my whole life that was of anymore significance than fathering three human beings? Once they didn't exist; now they live, they hurt and heal and love and laugh; they make mistakes and weave magic; they will bring children into the world and celebrate and mourn…

"That counts, ultimately, I know it does, and I'm determined to give my fathering its due."

—ELIOT A. DALEY
From "I'd Rather Be a Father", *Reader's Digest*

Being a father
Is quite a bother
But I like it, rather.

—OGDEN NASH

DADDIES

Daddies hold babies, push strollers, read stories.
Daddies have hands to hold, hugs,
kisses to tickle, and giggles.
Daddies teach us how to catch and kick and throw,
win and lose.
Daddies take us to parties, to the zoo.
Daddies need hugs and kisses, tickles,
jokes and giggles and "I love you."

—A. GREENSPUN

"After getting my first chance to change your diaper, I brought you back downstairs. I turned on the television, and as luck would have it, the San Francisco 49ers were playing.... I turned out all the lights, lay down on the couch, and put you on my chest. I was so afraid that my big hands were going to drop you, but I held on. It wasn't five minutes later that you fell asleep, holding my finger.... It was at that moment I realized that I was a dad."

—JOHN BARNET
Quoted in *Parents* magazine

"You worked so hard to make it up each step of the slide. Your tongue stuck out as you concentrated to keep your balance.... You looked toward me, asking for help, but I knew you could do it by yourself. I was right underneath you—you know your daddy would never let you fall."

—TOBY HAIR
Quoted in *Parents* magazine

"A leader is a man who does not groan under burdens, but takes them as a matter of course, allows them, tolerates them—and with a dash of humor. He knows how to keep his mouth shut about his difficulties and how to live a day at a time, doing quietly what needs doing at the moment. People will follow that sort of man."

—ELISABETH ELLIOT
From *Mark of a Man*

"Blessed is the man who fears the LORD, who finds great delight in his commands. His children will be mighty in the land; the generation of the upright will be blessed."

—PSALM 112:1-2 (NIV)

"If you look at some of the negative trends most on people's minds today—teenage pregnancy, children in poverty, educational failure or juvenile delinquency—the trend of fatherlessness is the engine that drives these pressing problems."

—DR. WADE HORN
From a Dallas newspaper report

"Fathering is unpredictable, untidy and frequently confusing. That is why there are so many fathers who have children, but so few children who have fathers."

—TIM HANSEL
From *What Kids Need Most in a Dad*

"You thought maybe God called himself 'Father' after you, to give you an illustration of what He's like? No way. He decided to call you 'father' after Him, to give you an illustration of what you're to be like as a father—copy."

—ANNE ORTLUND
From *A Man and His Loves*

"The man who lets his children take second place to his work will live to regret it."

—AUTHOR UNKNOWN
From Croft M. Pentz's *The Complete Book of Zingers*

"You know that the rulers of the Gentiles lord it over them, and their great men exercise authority over them. It is not so among you, but whoever wishes to be great among you shall be your servant."

—MATTHEW 20:25-26

THE
WARRIOR

(PROTECTOR)

"I saw heaven opened; and behold, a white horse,
and He who sat upon it is called Faithful and True;
and in righteousness he judges
and wages war."

REVELATION 19:11

T he final pages of Scripture describe Jesus at the end of time. Our Lord is astride a white war horse. His eyes are a flame of fire. His robe is spattered with blood. He carries a sharp sword. On his thigh He has a name written—King of Kings and Lord of Lords. He is called "Faithful and True and in righteousness He...wages war" (Revelation 19:11). Our Lord is a warrior!

Warriors face off with evil. Jesus, the ultimate warrior, came from a long line of warriors. On the first page of the New Testament He is called the Son of David. I think Jesus loved that title, probably for a variety of reasons. He certainly loved David's heart—and David had a warrior's heart. David stood alone against the champion of evil and the enemy of his people.

On that fateful day in the Valley of Elah it was David who became the "man of the in-between." It should have been Saul. Saul was the king and designated champion of

Israel who stood "head and shoulders above his people." Saul should have faced off with the giant. It was Saul whose stature filled the armor, and by all rights, it was Saul who should have met the champion of Philistia in the valley between the opposing armies. He was the one who should have left the ridge where the armies of Israel were encamped.

But he wouldn't. He stayed in his tent. He didn't have the warrior's heart. It took a boy to show that heart.

David became the man of the in-between. "I come to you in the name of the LORD of hosts," he had shouted that day to the champion of Philistia's evil kingdom. And the rest, as they say, is history. A thousand years later, the Greater Son of David met the Champion of Evil on a hill called Golgotha. His shout of victory was simple and to the point: "It is finished!" He had accomplished all that the Father had sent him to do.

How about you? Are you a warrior? Are you a man of

the in-between? Do you stand between those you love and all that would harm them? There is a warrior in every man's chest, a shield, a defender. One who remains alert on post, vigilant and protective.

A warrior out of balance, however, is a disastrous thing. A warrior out of balance protects nothing, and his family experiences pain, abuse, cruelty, and fear. Such a man is merely a brute, even more pitiful than a warrior who cowers, refusing to contend at all.

The true warrior is a protector. Whether he's stepping on intruding bugs or checking out the sounds that go "bump" in the night. Whether he's confronting a habitually abusive Little League coach or shining a flashlight into a spooky basement. Whether he's questioning an inappropriate television program or firmly removing explicit music from his home. Whether he's shoveling snow or helping women and children into a lifeboat on the Titanic. Men stand tallest when they are protecting and defending. And it is in the areas of soul and spirit that our families need most careful protection.

Be a warrior, yes.

But make sure you're a Tender Warrior.

"Behold, children are a gift of the LORD; the fruit of the womb is a reward. Like arrows in the hand of a warrior, so are the children of one's youth. How blessed is the man whose quiver is full of them; they shall not be ashamed, when they speak with their enemies in the gate."

—PSALM 127:4-5

"Never, never, never, never give up."

—WINSTON CHURCHILL

"A man's usefulness depends upon his living up to his ideals insofar as he can. It is hard to fail but it is worse never to have tried to succeed. All daring and courage, all iron endurance of misfortune, make for a finer, nobler type of manhood. Only those are fit to live who do not fear to die, and none are fit to die who have shrunk from the joy of the life and the duty of life."

—THEODORE ROOSEVELT

"For men to be men, we must regain the spirit of manhood in virility and integrity, the power of manhood in productivity and leadership, and the conviction of manhood in resolve and moral excellence."

—EDWIN LOUIS COLE
From *Tough Men for Tough Times*

"Who hath not served cannot command."

—JOHN FLOVIO

"The only thing necessary for the triumph of evil is for good men to do nothing."

—EDMUND BURKE

God give us men! A time like this demands
Strong minds, great hearts, true faith, and ready hands;
Men whom the lust of office does not kill;
Men whom the spoils of office cannot buy;
Men who possess opinions and a will;
Men who have honor; men who will not lie.

—JOSIAH GILBERT HOLLAND, 1819-1881
From *Wanted*, 1862

"Every climber who starts up the side of a mountain realizes that falling is a risk of climbing. He may fear the inevitable fall, and do everything within his power to avoid it, but he can't eliminate the possibility of it if he is committed to the climb."

—TIM KIMMEL
From *Little House on the Freeway*

GREAT MEN

Not gold, but only man can make
A people great and strong;
Men who, for truth and honor's sake,
Stand fast and suffer long.
Brave men who work while others sleep,
Who dare while others fly—
They build a nation's pillars deep
And lift them to the sky.

—RALPH WALDO EMERSON

TRUE NOBILITY

Who does his task from day to day
And meets whatever comes his way,
Believing God has willed it so,
Has found real greatness here below.
Who guards his post, no matter where,
Believing God must need him there,
Although but lowly toil it be,
Has risen to nobility.
For great and low there's but one test:
' Tis that each man shall do his best.
Who works with all the strength he can
Shall never die in debt to man.

—EDGAR GUEST

"The glory of young men is their strength; of old men, their experiences."

—PROVERBS 20:29

"By profession I am a soldier and take pride in that fact.
But I am prouder—infinitely prouder—to be a father."

—GEN. DOUGLAS MACARTHUR
From *Father, the Figure and the Force*

"We do not war according to the flesh, for the weapons
of our warfare are not of the flesh, but divinely powerful for the destruction of fortresses. We are destroying
speculations and every lofty thing raised up against the
knowledge of God and we are taking every thought cap-
tive to the obedience of Christ.

—2 CORINTHIANS 10:3-5

"Our very survival as a people will depend on the presence or absence of masculine leadership in millions of
homes."

—DR. JAMES DOBSON

"The youth board realized it had penetrated into a world
where there is no father. The welfare world of New York
is a fatherless world."

—AUTHOR UNKNOWN
From *New York Times Magazine*

"The principal danger to fatherhood today is that fathers do not have the vital sense of father power that they have had in the past. Because of a host of pressures from society, the father has lost the confidence that he is naturally important to his children—that he has the power to affect children, guide them, help them grow. He isn't confident that fatherhood is a basic part of being masculine and the legitimate focus of his life."

—DR. HENRY BILLER

"I hope you know how much I love you. The three of you have become the most important reason for my being on this earth.... I could be rich and famous and have everything I desire but without you my life would be meaningless, my heart would be empty, and I would not want to live. The three of you are my immortality.... I am a father who knows his children love him and that makes me a very lucky man!"

—GEN. NORMAN SCHWARZKOPF

Letter written to his children at midnight, just before the launching of the Gulf War offensive at 2:30 A.M.; from *It Doesn't Take a Hero*

Then out spake brave Horatius,
The captain of the gate:
"To every man upon this earth
Death cometh soon or late.
And how can man die better
Than facing fearful odds,
For the ashes of his fathers
And the temple of his gods?"

—FROM "HORATIUS AT THE GATE"
As retold by James Baldwin in William Bennett's *The Book of Virtues*

You cannot choose your battlefield,
God does that for you;
But you can plant a standard
Where a standard never flew.

—STEPHEN CRANE
From "The Colors"

"We have good corporals and good sergeants and some good lieutenants and captains. And those are far more important that good generals."

—WILLIAM TECUMSEH SHERMAN

MEDAL OF HONOR

"The Medal of Honor is America's highest award for military valor. It is bestowed on those who have performed an act of such conspicuous gallantry as to rise 'above and beyond the call of duty.' Indeed, the roll of honor includes 3,394 of the tens of millions of men and women who have served their country in the time of need since the Civil War. Yet among them are the names of generals and privates alike, of soldiers, sailors, marines, and airmen, of Americans of every color and creed, from every corner of this vast land. As a symbol of heroism, it has no equal in American life....

"[The Medal honors] a vital truth that war is waged and won or lost by individual men. Great armies, clever strategies, industrial might, all contribute to the success of a nation in war. On the battlefield, though, the ordinary soldiers more often than not turn the odds to victory. The Medal of Honor is bestowed on a man for his personal valor; it symbolizes the gratitude America feels when that soldier finds it within himself to perform with extraordinary courage.

"Beyond its personal meaning, the medal over the years has acquired another import: By recognizing the few it also recognizes the courage and sacrifice of all good American soldiers. This representative nature of the award by implication attributes gallantry to men other than those who receive it, men whose names are not found in books and are not portrayed in motion pictures but who have also put their lives on the line for their country.

"This is especially brought home by the custom of choosing for a Medal of Honor one of the unknown soldiers of each American conflict. The Unknown Soldier's sacrifice stands for that of many. In honoring the courage of one who lies nameless, the nation honors the courage of all who have served above and beyond the call of duty."

—BOSTON PUBLISHING COMPANY

If your officer's dead and the sergeants look white,
Remember, it's ruin to run from a fight;
So take open order, lie down, and sit tight,
An' wait for supports like a soldier.

—RUDYARD KIPLING
"The Young British Soldier"

"We have discovered that the scheme of 'outlawing war' has made war more like an outlaw without making it less frequent and that to banish the knight does not alleviate the suffering of the peasant."

—C.S. LEWIS
From *English Literature in the Sixteenth Century*

"There are several things worse than war, and they all come with losing one."

—AUTHOR UNKNOWN
Small sign at entrance of 5th SFG—Green Beret—
Headquarters, Nha Trang, Vietnam

"Any danger spot is tenable if men—brave men—will make it so."

—PRESIDENT JOHN F. KENNEDY

"Hal Moore was the last man to come out of the battle. It was the biggest battle he had ever fought. He was a lieutenant colonel, and he carried himself like a proud man. His sergeant major was at his side. It would need a Shakespeare to describe what happened then, but it was something that was love and manliness and pride. It was the moment of the brave. Hal Moore turned and went from group to group of his men, and only a few bothered to get up because there was no exclusivity now, no rank, and Hal Moore did not want them to stand and salute. He was saluting them. He talked with them. He thanked them. He was not solemn, and he did not bring to his greetings the salutations of a politician. There was no poverty of spirit in his handshake, and he shook every man's hand. It was a union of the men who had met and defeated the enemy, not forever, not in a victory that ended the war, but in a victory over their uncertainty. When their hour had come they had done their job, and it was that thought, too, that Hal Moore had in his mind. And he said that if they had won no one else's gratitude, they had his."

—DEAN BRELIS
From *The Face of South Vietnam*

When first under fire and you're wishful to duck,
Don't look or take heed at the man that is struck,
Be thankful you're living and trust to your luck,
And march to your front like a soldier.

—RUDYARD KIPLING
"The Young British Soldier"

"A brave Captain is as a root, out of which as branches the courage of his soldiers doth spring."

—SIR PHILLIP SIDNEY

"Unconditional love is the basis for every parenting decision and action. It is the driving force behind all discipline."

—DR. RAY GUARENDI
From *Back to the Family*

"You don't raise heroes, you raise sons. And if you treat them like sons, they'll turn out to be heroes, even if it's just in your own eyes."

— WALTER SCHIRRA, SENIOR
Quoted in *This Week*, February 3, 1963

"It doesn't take a hero to order men into battle. It takes a hero to be one of those men who goes into battle."

— GEN. NORMAN SCHWARZKOPF
From March 15, 1991, interview with Barbara Walters

"Fathers, a whole person, provide a sense of security for their children in both emotional and material ways. They are central to the development of their children, who need their love and support."

— MARK AND WANDA SINGER
From *Real Men Enjoy Their Kids*

"The LORD your God carried you, as a father carries his son, all the way you went until you reached this place."

— DEUTERONOMY 1:31 (NIV)

"Many kids, especially younger ones, believe their earthly dad is nearly invincible. How much greater must their heavenly Father be if their earthly dad prays to Him!"

—KEN CANFIELD
From "Safe in a Father's Love," *Charisma*

"Risk failure because the risk is worth it. Dive in and challenge your fear of inadequacy. You're going to have to face it throughout the fathering process, so it's in your own best interest to become accustomed to challenging it."

—BRIAN NEWMAN
From *The Father Book*

"My bereavement reflected primarily my failure to begin to comprehend, let alone fully to do so, that evolution of loyalties that accompanies marriage—and should do so. Christopher was now wedded and had a child. He is devoted to his wife, and understandably so; and about his daughter, he is quite simply cuckoo, also understandable. Day-to-day closeness of the kind we had was becoming a drain, distracting to the primary emotional and psychological demands he was feeling. I was wrong in supposing that the nature of a relationship that had proved airborne in his teens and in his twenties could hope to continue into married life. The rift, however painful, almost certainly had to come, and had to be painful, there being no anesthetic for extractions of this kind."

—WILLIAM F. BUCKLEY, JR.
From *Windfall*

"Tell a man he is brave, and you help him to become so."

—THOMAS CARLYLE

"Have courage for the great sorrows of life and patience for the small ones; and when you have laboriously accomplished your daily task, go to sleep in peace. God is awake."

—VICTOR HUGO

"I'm constantly amazed by the number of people who can't seem to control their own schedules. Over the years, I've had many executives come to me and say with pride: 'Boy, last year I worked so hard that I didn't take any vacation.' It's actually nothing to be proud of. I always feel like responding: 'You dummy. You mean to tell me that you can take responsibility for an $80 million project and you can't plan two weeks out of the year to go off with your family and have some fun?'

"If you want to make good use of your time, you've got to know what's most important and then give it all you've got."

—LEE IACOCCA
From *Iacocca: An Autobiography*

"A little four-year-old girl became frightened late one night during a thunderstorm. After one particularly loud clap of thunder, she jumped up from her bed, ran down the hall, and burst into her parents' room. Jumping right in the middle of the bed, she sought out her parents' arms for comfort and assurance. 'Don't worry, Honey,' her father said, trying to calm her fear. 'The Lord will protect you.' The little girl snuggled closer to her father and said, 'I know that, Daddy, but right now I need someone with skin on!'

"The honesty of some children! This little one did not doubt her heavenly Father's ability to protect her, but she was also aware that He had given her an earthly father she could run to: someone whom God had entrusted with a special gift that could bring her comfort, security, and personal acceptance—the blessing of meaningful touch."

—GARY SMALLEY AND JOHN TRENT
From *The Gift of the Blessing*

"Never sacrifice the permanent on the altar of the immediate."

—BOB KRANING

"Keep out of your child's life anything that will keep Christ out of his heart."

—AUTHOR UNKNOWN
From Croft M. Pentz's *The Complete Book of Zingers*

"Once we gathered as a family to discuss the use of television in our home. Much reading and research had convinced me that we Americans in general, and my family in particular, were spending too much time in front of a TV and letting our minds atrophy. I knew exactly what would happen, however, if I presented this information to my family in the form of an arbitrary limitation on TV viewing: screaming, complaining, and harsh withdrawal symptoms.

"Instead we met together in a family counsel and discussed some of the data about what is happening to families because of TV and what values are being espoused in many shows. I explained how some people regard TV as an open cesspool in their homes or a plug-in drug that can have a powerful, though subtle, influence. To emphasize my point, I even shared Alexander Pope's well-known statement concerning vice:

> 'Vice is a monster of so frightful mien,
> As to be hated needs but to be seen;
> Yet seen too oft, familiar with her face,

We first endure, then pity, then embrace.'

"Our discussion ended with a decision to try to limit ourselves to about one hour of TV a day—good entertainment and education. Obviously we've not always reached that goal; but when we have, the results have been spectacular. Homework has been done more completely and more conscientiously. Reading, thinking, analyzing, and creating have replaced viewing."

—STEPHEN COVEY
From *Principle-Centered Leadership*

"As arrows in the hand of a warrior, so are the children of one's youth. How blessed is the man whose quiver is full of them."

—PSALM 127:4-5

"If we must perish in the fight, Oh! let us die like men."

—GEORGE WASHINGTON PATTEN

"If all men were just, there would be no need of valor."

—AGESILAUS, 444-400 B.C.

FELLOWSHIP OF THE UNASHAMED

"I am part of the 'Fellowship of the Unashamed.' The die has been cast. The decision has been made. I have stepped over the line. I won't look back, let up, slow down, back away or be still.

"My past is redeemed, my present makes sense, and my future is secure. I'm finished and done with low living, sight walking, small planning, smooth knees, colorless dreams, tamed visions, mundane talking, cheap giving, and dwarfed goals.

"I no longer need preeminence, prosperity, position, promotions, plaudits or popularity. I don't have to be right, first, tops, recognized, praised, regarded or rewarded. I now live by faith, lean on His presence, love with patience, live by prayer and labor with power.

"My face is set, my gait is fast, my goal is heaven, my road is narrow, my way is rough, my companions are few, my Guide is reliable, and my mission is clear. I cannot be bought, compromised, detoured, lured away, turned back, deluded or delayed. I will not flinch in the face of sacrifice, hesitate in the presence of adversity, negotiate at the table of the enemy, ponder at the pool of popularity or meander in the maze of mediocrity.

"I won't give up, shut up, let up or slow up until I have stayed up, store up, prayed up, paid up and spoken up for the cause of Christ. I am a disciple of Jesus. I must go till He comes, give till I drop, preach till all know and work till He stops me. And when He comes for His own, He will have no problem recognizing me. My banner is clear: I am part of the 'Fellowship of the Unashamed.' "

—BOB MOOREHEAD
Used by permission

"A few honest men are better than numbers."

—OLIVER CROMWELL

"Temptation rarely comes in working hours. It is in their leisure time that men are made or marred."

—W.T. TAYLOR

"Above all else, guard your heart, for it is the wellspring of life."

—PROVERBS 4:23 (NIV)

"Faith is trusting God to satisfy when I am weaning myself from unhealthy but enjoyable pacifiers: workaholism, perfectionism, fantasy life, overly dependent relationships."

—PAMELA REEVE
From *Faith Is*

"We never understand how little we need in this world until we know the loss of it."

—SIR JAMES MATTHEW BARRIE AND MARGARET OGILVY (1896)

"There needs to be a clear distinction between discipline and abuse. Disciplining a child does not give license for venting anger or for extreme and unfair correction. True discipline confirms a parent's love for the child. They care enough to set healthy limits and to enforce the rules of good conduct and character."

—HENRY GARIEPY
From *Wisdom to Live By*

"A child that is allowed to be disrespectful to his parents will not have true respect for anyone."

—AUTHOR UNKNOWN
From Croft M. Pentz's *The Complete Book of Zingers*

"...If we stand idly by, if we seek merely swollen, slothful ease, and ignoble peace, if we shrink from the hard contests where men must win at hazard of their lives and at the risk of all they hold dear, then the bolder and stronger peoples will pass us by and will win for themselves the domination of the world. Let us therefore boldly face the life of strife, resolute to do our duty well and manfully; resolute to uphold righteousness by deed and by word; resolute to be both honest and brave, to serve high ideals..."

—THEODORE ROOSEVELT

OUR HEROES

Here's a hand to the boy who has courage
To do what he knows to be right;
When he falls in the way of temptation,
He has a hard battle to fight.
Who strives against self and his comrades
Will find a most powerful foe.
All honor to him if he conquers.
A cheer for the boy who says "NO!"
There's many a battle fought daily
The world knows nothing about;
There's many a brave little soldier
Whose strength puts a legion to rout.
And he who fights sin single-handed
Is more of a hero, I say,
Than he who leads soldiers to battle
And conquers by arms in the fray.
Be steadfast, my boy, when you're tempted,
To do what you know to be right.
Stand firm by the colors of manhood,
And you will o'ercome in the fight.

"The right," be your battle cry ever
In waging the warfare of life,
And God, who knows who are the heroes,
Will give you the strength for the strife.

—PHOEBE CARY

"…We shall go on to the end, we shall fight in France, we shall fight on the seas and oceans, we shall fight with growing confidence and growing strength in the air, we shall defend our island, whatever the cost may be, we shall fight on the beaches, we shall fight on the landing grounds, we shall fight in the fields and in the streets, we shall fight in the hills; we shall never surrender, and even if, which I do not for a moment believe, this island or a large part of it were subjugated and starving, then our Empire beyond the seas, armed and guarded by the British fleet, would carry on the struggle, until, in God's good time, the New World, with all its power and might, steps forth to the rescue and the liberation of the old."

—WINSTON CHURCHILL

TRY, TRY AGAIN

'Tis a lesson you should heed,

Try, try again;

If at first you don't succeed,

Try, try again;

Then your courage should appear,

For, if you will persevere,

You will conquer, never fear;

Try, try again.

—AUTHOR UNKNOWN

LETTER FROM A PRESIDENT

To Mrs. Bixby, Boston, Mass.

Dear Madam,

I have been shown in the files of the War Department a statement of the Adjutant General of Massachusetts that you are the mother of five sons who have died gloriously on the field of battle. I feel how weak and fruitless must be any word of mine which should attempt to beguile you from the grief of a loss so overwhelming. But I cannot refrain from tendering you the consolation that may

be found in the thanks of the republic they died to save.
I pray that our Heavenly Father may assuage the
anguish of your bereavement, and leave you only the
cherished memory of the loved and lost, and the solemn
pride that must be yours to have laid so costly a sacrifice
upon the altar of freedom.

Yours very sincerely and respectfully,

—ABRAHAM LINCOLN
From William Bennett's *The Book of Virtues*

And when with grief you see your brother stray,
Or in a night of error lose his way,
Direct his wandering and restore the day…
Leave to avenging Heaven his stubborn will.
For O, remember, he is your brother still.

—JONATHAN SWIFT

"Be kind; everyone you meet is fighting a hard battle."

—JOHN WATSON

YOU MUSTN'T QUIT

When things go wrong, as they sometimes will,
When the road you're trudging seems all uphill,
When the funds are low and the debts are high
And you want to smile, but you have to sigh,
When care is pressing you down a bit,
Rest! if you must—but never quit.

Life is queer, with its twists and turns,
As every one of us sometimes learns,
And many a failure turns about
When he might have won if he'd stuck it out;
Stick to your task, though the pace seems slow—
You may succeed with one more blow.

Success is failure turned inside out—
The silver tint of the clouds of doubt—
And you never can tell how close you are,
It may be near when it seems afar;
So stick to the fight when you're hardest hit—
It's when things seem worst that YOU MUSTN'T QUIT.

—AUTHOR UNKNOWN

"Gentlemen may cry, peace, peace—but there is no peace. The war is actually begun! The next gale that sweeps from the north will bring to our ears the clash of resounding arms! Our brethren are already in the field! Why stand we here idle? What is it that gentlemen wish? What would they have? Is life so dear, or peace so sweet, as to be purchased at the price of chains and slavery? Forbid it, Almighty God! I know not what course others may take; but as for me, give me liberty, or give me death!"

—PATRICK HENRY

"Since we have such a huge crowd of men of faith watching us from the grandstands, let us strip off anything that slows us down or holds us back…and let us run with patience the particular race God has set before us."

—HEBREWS 12:1 (TLB)

RESULTS AND ROSES

The man who wants a garden fair,
Or small or very big,
With flowers growing here and there,
Must bend his back and dig.
The things are mighty few on earth
That wishes can attain.
Whate'er we want of any worth
We've got to work to gain.
It matters not what goal you seek
Its secret here reposes:
You've got to dig from week to week
To get Results or Roses.

—EDGAR GUEST

"My father's saber was a sacred thing in our family. We called it his West Point sword because he'd gotten it the year he graduated in 1917. 'Duty, Honor, Country,' the West Point motto, was his creed, and it became mine."

—GEN. NORMAN SCHWARZKOPF
From *It Doesn't Take a Hero*

"Those who do not do battle for their country do not know with what ease they accept their citizenship in America."

—DEAN BRELIS
From *The Face of South Vietnam*

This story shall the good man teach his son;
And Crispin Crispian shall ne'er go by,
From this day to the ending of the world,
But we in it shall be remembered,
We few, we happy few, we band of brothers.
For he to-day that sheds his blood with me
Shall be my brother; be he ne'er so vile,
This day shall gentle his condition;
And gentlemen in England now a-bed
Shall think themselves accursed they were not here,
And hold their manhoods cheap whiles any speaks
That fought with us upon Saint Crispin's day.

—WILLIAM SHAKESPEARE
From *Henry V*

"World War II pilot George Leonard asked a group of Army Green Berets how they define 'the ideal warrior': They cited loyalty, patience, intensity, calmness, compassion and will. They agreed that the true warrior knows himself, knows his limitations.... Self-mastery, according to the Special Forces men, is a warrior's central motivation. He is always practicing, always seeking to hone his skills, so as to become the best possible instrument for accomplishing his mission. The warrior takes calculated risks and tests himself repeatedly. He believes in something greater than himself: a religion, a cause. He does not worship violence, but he is at home with it. He may snivel (their word for complain), but he is not a victim."

—GORDON DALBEY
From *Healing the Masculine Soul*

"Be on the alert, stand firm in the faith, act like men, be strong. Let all that you do be done in love."

—1 CORINTHIANS 16:13

"As David's time to die drew near, he charged Solomon his son, saying, 'I am going the way of all the earth. *Be strong, therefore, and show yourself a man.* And keep the charge of the LORD your God, to walk in His ways, to keep His statutes, His commandments, His ordinances, and His testimonies, according to what is written in the law of Moses, that you may succeed in all that you do and wherever you turn.' "

— 1 KINGS 2:1-3 (EMPHASIS ADDED)

"Honest mistakes made by loving parents do not damage children psychologically, not now or at some unknown juncture years down the road. They may make life a little tougher for a while, for all involved, but they don't ruin 'psyches.' Kids were built to withstand being raised by human beings, with all of our shortcomings and inconsistencies."

— DR. RAY GUARENDI
From *Back to the Family*

"We need passion. We need challenge and risk. We need to be pushed to our limit. And I believe this is just what happens when we accept a warrior's code, when we try to live each moment as a warrior, whether in education, job, marriage, child rearing, or recreation. The truth is that we don't have to go to combat to go to war. Life is fired at us like a bullet, and there is no escaping it short of death. All escape attempts—drugs, aimless travel, the distractions of the media, empty material pursuits—are sure to fail in the long run, as more and more of us are beginning to learn."

—GEORGE LEONARD
Quoted by Gordon Dalbey in *Healing the Masculine Soul*

"The present time of the highest importance—it is time to wake up to reality…The night is nearly over; the day has almost dawned…Let us arm ourselves for the fight of the day!"

—ROMANS 13:11-12 (PHILLIPS)

"A lord summoned a monk and asked him to devise a koan celebrating his family. The monk went off to contemplate, and returned, presenting the lord with a scroll upon which were the words:

> Grandfather dies,
>
> Father dies,
>
> Son dies.

"The lord was furious. 'I ask you to give me something to express my joy, and you bring me this?' He was about to order a soldier to behead the monk when the monk said, 'No father lives longer than his son. Therein lies truest happiness.'

"The lord ordered the soldier to sheath his sword."

—WILLIAM F. BUCKLEY, JR.
From *Windfall*

"When alone, guard your thoughts; in the family guard your temper; in company guard your words."

—AUTHOR UNKNOWN
From Croft M. Pentz's *The Complete Book of Zingers*

THE
MENTOR

(TEACHER)

"Come, you children, listen to me;
I will teach you the fear of the LORD."

PSALM 34:11

Sometimes it's a grandpa with his favorite whittlin' knife showing his little buddy how to carve his initials in a block of wood. Sometimes it's a dad playin' catch with a young son. Sometimes it's a daddy and his little princess talking about why "the girls down the street are acting weird." Sometimes it's a determined twosome on a Saturday in the garage, with dirty hands, oil-smeared faces, and laughter—lots of laughter—tearing the daylights out of a lawnmower that refuses to run. Sometimes it's the father of the bride working through a young lady's last-minute jitters—and sternly holding his own emotions in check.

Together. Always together.

Whatever the situation, it's the mentor in a man reaching out with the heart of a sage to teach life to those he loves most. Men are supposed to know about life. And teach it. There is a mentor in every man's heart.

I'll never forget the most significant table game of my life. I was just a little guy. My heart had been full for days, anticipating an upcoming stay with my grandpa and grandma at their place. I was the apple of their eye (and I knew it). When I was with Grandpa, I was a little "king for a day." Man, it was great! Ice cream…walks in the woods…wind in the trees…birds singing…and, of course, Grandpa's ever-present Pepsi Cola®! Life just didn't get any better.

And then, at the end of the day, just before lights out, Grandpa and Grandma would submit to "just one more" round of Parcheesi at the yellow Formica table, with awkward stainless steel legs, in the kitchen. A board, dice, competition, and sometimes…the thrill of victory! Sometimes it was nip and tuck. This particular time I was running behind, and there's something in a little boy that can't stand the thought of getting whipped by his own grandma. So I did what I suppose a lot of other youngsters have done in similar circumstances.

I cheated.

Big mistake.

But I learned more that night about life and being a man than any other month of nights combined. I wasn't a very subtle or effective cheater (and pray I never become one), and was easily caught in the act. To this day, I can still see the expression on their faces. Glasses pushed down over the end of their noses, eyes peering over bifocals into my eyes. I can still see the pain on their faces. And I can still feel the anguish of my failure, of letting them down. You've probably been there, too.

Grandma didn't say anything at all, and Grandpa didn't say much. Just a few simple words. But what words! Their wisdom and gentle power impacted me for a lifetime.

"Stu," he said quietly, "you're a Weber boy. And Weber boys don't lie or cheat."

Oh my! Think of it. There in a little kitchen many years

ago, a man now long gone touched me in a way that still grips me at the very center. He defined life for me.

My grandpa loved me enough that night to help me establish my identity. In just a phrase or two, he had given definition to my life, my character, my masculinity, and my family. You talk about wisdom, guidance, and direction! There was a whole boatload, enough for a lifetime. From the lips of a simple coal miner. In a quiet moment. Across a Parcheesi board.

Such moments cannot be programmed or scheduled. They don't rise from an agenda. They are the quality times that rise spontaneously out of great deliberate quantities of time spent in relationship. I don't think my grandpa had ever heard the word "mentor" in those days. But he was a man. And he had a heart. I'm so glad he gave it to me. There is a mentor in every man's chest.

"This man whose body lies before me was not only my father and my friend, but he was also the source of great inspiration for me.... When I was between ten and thirteen years of age, my dad and I would arise very early before the sun came up on a wintry morning. We would put on our hunting clothes and heavy boots,...[and] we would await the arrival of the sun and the awakening of the animal world.... Something dramatic...occurred out there in the forest between my dad and me. An intense love and affection was generated on those mornings that set the tone for a lifetime of fellowship. There was a closeness and a oneness that made me want to be like that man...that made me choose his values as my values, his dreams as my dreams, his God as my God."

—DR. JAMES DOBSON
At the funeral of James Dobson, Senior, from *Straight Talk*

"To become a father is to...realize that the touches you make upon your son will shape him, for better or for worse, for his entire life."

—KENT NEWBORN
From *Letters to My Son*

"…Quality time depends on quantity time. The more time spent with or near a child—be it playing a game, drying dishes, or reading quietly in the same room—the more quality time is likely to occur."

—DR. RAY GUARENDI
From *Back to the Family*

"Mercifully, parenting is not an efficient process—the old concept of 'quality time' is a cruel cop-out. As a parent, he gets to hang out with his children, reliving the joys of his childhood. The play is the thing."

—FRANK S. PITTMAN III
From *Man Enough*

"Be reasonable—don't expect your youngsters to listen to your advice and ignore your example."

—AUTHOR UNKNOWN
From Croft M. Pentz's *The Complete Book of Zingers*

"The child you want to raise as an upright and honorable person requires a lot more of your time than your money."

—GEORGE VARKY

If I could do it all over again…
I'd like to make more mistakes.
I'd relax. I'd limber up.
I would be sillier than I was the first time.
I would take fewer things seriously.
I'd let them take more chances.
I'd let them have more fun.
I'd let them eat fewer carrots and more ice cream.
Maybe I'd have more actual troubles,
but I'd have fewer imaginary ones.

—RAY ORTLUND
From *A Man and His Loves*

"When an adult male truly understands the meaning of three words—time, commitment, and responsibility—then, in my opinion, he can call himself a father and a man."

—DR. WADE HORN
Clinical psychologist and director of the National Fatherhood Initiative

"Our children are living messages we send to a time and place we will never see."

—AUTHOR UNKNOWN

> Lives of great men all remind us
> We can make our lives sublime.
> And, departing, leave behind us
> Footprints on the sands of time.

—HENRY WADSWORTH LONGFELLOW
From "Psalm of Life"

"No one who reaches the end of his life has ever looked back and said, 'Oh, I wish I had spent more time at the office instead of with my kids.' "

—MIKE YORKEY
From *Daddy's Home*

"Household responsibilities are tools for building self-reliance, for making a youngster tackle jobs himself, without waiting for someone else to step in."

—DR. RAY GUARENDI
From *Back to the Family*

"The father-son relation is the basic link of continuity in life, carrying the male principle and the tradition of responsibility from one generation to the next."

—MAX LERNER
From *The Unfinished Country*

"The absence of the father or of his instruction leaves a void that may take years experience and many mistakes to overcome."

—DR. CHARLES STANLEY
From *Is There a Man in the House?*

"It is my God-appointed task to ensure that my sons will be ready to lead a family. I must equip them to that end. Little boys are the hope of the next generation. They are the fathers of tomorrow. They must know who they are and what they are to do. They must see their role model in action."

—STEVE FARRAR
From *Point Man*

"The absence of fathers is linked to most social nightmares—from boys with guns to girls with babies. No welfare reform plan can cut poverty as thoroughly as a two-parent family."

—JOSEPH P. SHAPIRO AND JOANNE M. SCHROF
From "Honor Thy Children," *U.S. News and World Report*, February 27, 1995

"A boy particularly needs to know his dad. Dad represents the man he will become—the husband he will be to his wife, the father he will be to his children, the provider he will be for his family, the leader he will be in his church, and the witness he will be in the world.... He needs a dad he can be proud of."

—RICHARD STRAUSS
From *Confident Children and How They Grow*

"Give me a young man in whom there is something of the old, and an old man with something of the young; guided so, a man may grow old in body, but never in mind."

—CICERO
From *De Senectute, XI*, quoted in *The Masculine Journey*

"I am a product of long corridors, empty sunlit rooms, upstairs indoor silences, attics explored in solicitude, distant noises of gurgling cisterns and pipes, and the noise of the wind under the tiles. Also, of endless books. My father bought all the books he read and never got rid of any of them. There were books in the study, books in the drawing room, books in the cloakroom, books (two deep) in the great bookcase on the landing, books in a bedroom, books piled as high as my shoulder in the cistern attic, books of all kinds reflecting every transient stage of my parents' interests.... In the seemingly endless rainy afternoons I took volume after volume from the shelves. I had always the same certainty of finding a book that was new to me as a man who walks into a field has of finding a new blade of grass."

—C.S. LEWIS
From *Surprised by Joy*

"Children should be taught more about the Rock of Ages instead of the ages of the rocks."

—AUTHOR UNKNOWN
From Croft M. Pentz's *The Complete Book of Zingers*

THE BOY SCOUT OATH

On my honor I will do my best
To do my duty to God and my country
and to obey the Scout Law;
To help other people at all times;
To keep myself physically strong,
mentally awake, and morally straight.

—AUTHOR UNKNOWN

"A man never starts to get old until he starts to forget his dream."

—LOUIS L'AMOUR

From *Hanging Woman Creek*

"Most men I know have an instinct for fatherhood that was triggered the day their first child was born. They innately recognized the No. 1 requirement of fatherhood: be there."

—FRED BARNES

From *The New Republic*, July 12, 1993

"You will take with you the satisfaction that proceeds from the consciousness of duty faithfully performed, and I earnestly pray that a Merciful God will extend to you his blessing and protection."

> —ROBERT E. LEE
> General, Confederate States Army

"My kids, hopefully, are learning through a transparent life that their dad has needs. Sometimes my need is to be forgiven—so I must be willing to admit failure and wrong. Then and only then do I become *real!* Do not fear that transparency will cause a child to lose respect for you."

> —CHARLES R. SWINDOLL
> From *The Strong Family*

"One way to correct your children is to correct the example you are setting for them."

> —AUTHOR UNKNOWN

"The child is the father of the man."

> —WILLIAM WORDSWORTH

"It was 10 P.M., time for bed. Freddy jumped under the covers and insisted we sleep in the same bed. 'Dad, dad, there's so much I want to tell you,' he said. He couldn't remember exactly what; he was fast asleep."

—FRED BARNES
From *The New Republic*, July 12, 1993

"Never being welcomed into the male world by older men is a wound in the chest. The police chief of Detroit remarked that the young men he arrests not only don't have any responsible older man in the house, they have never met one. When you look at a gang, you are looking, as Michael Meade remarked, at young men who have no older men around them at all."

—ROBERT BLY
From *Iron John*

THE ANVIL OF GOD'S WORD
Last eve I paused beside a blacksmith's door,
and heard the anvil ring the vesper chime;
Then looking in, I saw, upon the floor,
Old hammers, worn with beating years of time.

"How many anvils have you had," said I,

"To wear and batter all these hammers so?"

"Just one," said he, and then with twinkling eye,

"The anvil wears the hammers out, you know."

And so, I thought, the Anvil of God's Word,

For ages skeptic blows have beat upon,

Yet, though the noise of falling blows was heard,

The Anvil is unchanged, the hammers gone."

—JOHN CLIFFORD

"Spirituality is an umbrella which protects while it nurtures a family's well-being. It builds cohesiveness through shared beliefs and values. It empowers a parent to teach by example, the most durable form of childrearing. It provides comfort through faith in a Creator who can guide one's parenting."

—DR. RAY GUARENDI
From *Back to the Family*

"You are about as happy as you choose to be."

—ABRAHAM LINCOLN

"Let it be said firmly that the bogus humility represented by the 'we haven't got all the answers' line is as far from Christian virtue as lust is from love. And indeed it is inconceivable that anyone acquainted with the Gospels should speak as though our Lord Himself were incapable of the crisp, the pithy, the devastating comeback. Whatever else our Lord was accused of, He was not charged with preserving a sage and mystical silence while the weary, doubtful, dejected, and oppressed threw their tragically unanswered questions at him. Yet in every other religious journal one picks up today, one reads the amazing sentence, 'We must not talk as if we've got all the answers.'

"Why in God's name not? What is our Christian duty if not to make plain that in the Christian faith the gravest doubts and worries of men are richly answered? What do these prevaricators mean? Have we not got the answers in their eyes? Is our Lord untrustworthy, the church founded upon an eternal question mark, the faith a fog? It will be time enough to put this slogan on our banner when we have heard a dying martyr proclaim it as the surety of his hope. The scene is worth picturing. The flames gather around the stake, but the martyr's eyes are ablaze only with faith. 'I die gladly. I die at peace with God. My last message to you is this: We must not talk as if we've got all the answers.' "

—HARRY BLAMIRES
From *The Tyranny of Time*

"Fathers transmit their own style to their sons, consciously or otherwise."

—RAY ORTLUND
From *A Man and His Loves*

"Fathers, do not provoke your children to anger; but bring them up in the discipline and instruction of the Lord."

—EPHESIANS 6:4

"God gives enough evidence so that the believing heart can have certainty, but never so much evidence that the element of faith is eliminated."

—AUTHOR UNKNOWN

In truth thou canst not read the Scriptures too much;
And what thou readest,
thou canst not read too well;
And what thou readest well,
thou canst not too well understand;
And what thou understandest well,
thou canst not too well teach;
And what thou teachest well,
thou canst not too well live.

—MARTIN LUTHER

"When we come up against the enormity of God, it ought to cause us great wonder…and awe…and laughter!"

—RONALD BARCLAY ALLEN

"We need love's tender lessons taught as only weakness can; God hath his small interpreters; the child must teach the man."

—JOHN GREENLEAF WHITTIER

"I can't imagine a man really enjoying a book and reading it only once."

—C.S. LEWIS
From *The Letters of C.S. Lewis to Arthur Greeves*

Fight for a principle.
Express your gratitude.
Overcome an old fear.
Take two minutes to appreciate the beauty of nature.
Tell someone you love them.
Tell them again and again.

—AUTHOR UNKNOWN

"Wherein you reprove another be unblamable yourself, for example is more prevalent than precept."

—GEORGE WASHINGTON
From "The Rules of Civility"

"A man who has committed a mistake and doesn't correct it is committing another mistake."

—CONFUCIUS

"Treat no one with callous disregard. Children know when they are being taken seriously by others, and they imitate what they see. Therein lies both our hope and our peril."

—WILLIAM J. BENNETT
From *The Book of Virtues*

"Children have more need of models than of critics."

—JOSEPH JOUBERT
From *Proverbs to Live By*

"One consequence is worth one thousand words. Holding a child accountable for his behavior will teach him far more than will dozens of lectures, naggings, or threats."

—DR. RAY GUARENDI
From *Back to the Family*

"People have a way of becoming what you encourage them to be—not what you nag them to be."

—AUTHOR UNKNOWN

"I look at my children and I wish for them enough opposition to make them strong, enough insults to make them choose, enough hard decisions to make them see that following Jesus brings with it a cost—a cost eminently worth it, but still a cost."

—DON CARSON
From *Proverbs to Live By*

"He climbed onto the seat and positioned his feet on the pedals, his hands on the handle bars. 'Don't let go,' he ordered. 'I'll be right next to you,' I assured him. 'I won't let you fall....'

"I thought of the days ahead—of times when I would show my son balance, when I would run alongside him, when I would be there to hold him, and when I would have to let go again and again."

—MATTHEW NORQUIST
From "A Dad's Moment of Balance," *Focus on the Family*

"People who know little are usually great talkers, while men who know much say little."

—EMILE, DE L'EDUCATION

"When I was a boy of 14, my father was so ignorant I could hardly stand to have the old man around. But when I got to be 21, I was astounded at how much the old man had learned in seven years."

—SAMUEL L. CLEMENS

"Play has often been called a child's 'work.' But amid life in the fast lane these days, playtime with his children is part of a father's work too. Think of what 'play'—meaning any kind of pleasant interaction—accomplishes with a child of any age."

—PAUL LEWIS
From "Secrets of a Winning Dad," *Charisma*

"My wife and I view our children's bedtime as the most critical time of their daily routine. How we bring the daily clutter of events, emotions, and experiences to a conclusion has a big effect on how my children view themselves and the world in which they are attempting to live."

—TIM KIMMEL
From *Little House on the Freeway*

"But if any of you lacks wisdom, let him ask of God, who gives to all men generously and without reproach, and it will be given to him."

—JAMES 1:5

"Boys become men by watching men, by standing close to men. Manhood is a ritual passed from generation to generation with precious few spoken instructions. Passing the torch of manhood is a fragile, tedious task. If the rite of passage is successfully completed, the boy-become-man is like an oak of hardwood character. His shade and influence will bless all those who are fortunate enough to lean on him and rest under his canopy."

—PRESTON GILLHAM

"A man should never be ashamed to own he has been in the wrong, which is but saying in other words, that he is wiser today than he was yesterday."

—JONATHAN SWIFT

"A child's household chores may be accompanied by an allowance, but they are not done for an allowance. They are done because they need to be done."

—WILLIAM J. BENNETT
From *The Book of Virtues*

"Heavenly Father, help me by example and precept to build, in young lives entrusted to me, foundations of true wisdom that will stand the tests of life's perils and pitfalls."

—HENRY GARIEPY
From *Wisdom to Live By*

"Listen, my son, to your father's instruction and do not forsake your mother's teaching."

—PROVERBS 1:8 (NIV)

"What a father says to his children is not heard by the world, but it will be heard by posterity."

—JEAN PAUL RICHTER

"Teaching smaller children may focus on four-letter words such as duty, work, earn, give, and love."

—AUTHOR UNKNOWN
From Croft M. Pentz's *The Complete Book of Zingers*

"There are places in America where fathers—usually the best hope to socialize boys—are so rare that bedlam engulfs the community. Teachers, ministers, cops and other substitute authority figures fight losing battles in these places against gang members to present role models to preteen and teenage boys. The result is often an astonishing level of violence and incomprehensible incidents of brutality."

—JOSEPH P. SHAPIRO AND JOANNE M. SCHROF
From "Honor Thy Children," *U.S. News and World Report*,
February 27, 1995

"Respect the child. Be not too much his parent. Trespass not on his solitude."

—RALPH WALDO EMERSON

THE FARMER AND HIS SONS

"A farmer, being at death's door, and desiring to impart to his sons a secret of much moment, called them round him and said, 'My sons, I am shortly about to die. I would have you know, therefore, that in my vineyard there lies a hidden treasure. Dig, and you will find it.' As soon as their father was dead, the sons took spade and fork and turned up the soil of the vineyard over and over again, in their search for the treasure which they supposed to lie buried there. They found none, however: but the vines, after so thorough a digging, produced a crop such as had never before been seen.

"There is no treasure without toil."

—AESOP

"A man of knowledge uses words with restraint and a man of understanding is even-tempered."

—PROVERBS 17:27 (NIV)

"Eating words has never given me indigestion."

—WINSTON CHURCHILL

Write a letter to someone who misses you.

Encourage a youth who has lost faith.

Keep a promise.

Forget an old grudge.

Examine your demands on others

and vow to reduce them.

— AUTHOR UNKNOWN
From the *Heartland Sampler Calendar*

"To carry the feelings of childhood into the powers of manhood, to combine the child's sense of wonder and novelty with the appearances, which every day for perhaps forty years had rendered familiar...this is the character of genius."

— HOLBROOK JACKSON

"Walk a little plainer, Daddy! I know that once you walked this way many years ago, and what you did along the way I'd really like to know; for sometimes when I am tempted, I don't know what to do. So walk a little plainer, Daddy, for I must follow you."

— AUTHOR UNKNOWN

"A man can fail many times, but he isn't a failure until he begins to blame somebody else."

—JOHN BURROUGHS

"A child tells in the street what his father says at home."

—AUTHOR UNKNOWN
From the Talmud

DAD AND ME TOGETHER

Dad told me that old adage,
About the birds, 'Birds of a feather,'
And I kept thinking while we walked,
Dad and me together.

—OTTIS SHIRK
From *The Family Album*

"Dad is the vehicle through which she arrives at the understanding of her value."

—H. NORMAN WRIGHT
From *Always Daddy's Girl*

"The first man in every woman's life is her father. How she views the men she meets later, how she values herself, depends to some extent on her relationship with her dad."

—MYRNA BLYTH
From *The Ladies Home Journal*

"Household chores, homework, extracurricular activities, after-school jobs, and volunteer work all contribute to maturation if parental example and expectations are clear, consistent, and commensurate with the developing powers of the child."

—WILLIAM J. BENNETT
From *The Book of Virtues*

Is he not your father who formed you?
Did he not make you and establish you?
Remember the days of old,
think of the generations long ago;
ask your father to recount it
and your elders to tell you the tale.

—DEUTERONOMY 32:6-7 (NEB)

"I remember walking around the block with Dad, and he told me, 'Think big about your life. Have big dreams! Have God-sized expectations!' "

—AUTHOR UNKNOWN
From *A Man and His Loves*

"Even golf is a trifling thing beside the privilege of taking a small son to the zoo and letting him see his first lion, his first tiger and best of all, his first elephant. Probably he will think they are part of your own handiwork turned out for his pleasure."

—HEYWOOD BROUN
From "Holding a Baby," *Reader's Digest*, July 1941

"The mystery of feeling your father in you hints at the great mystery of the Father God's longing to fill men with His Spirit."

—GORDON DALBY
From *Father and Son*

"If there are times when it seems as if everyone is staring at your child and at you, they are. But—and this is what's important—most of these onlookers aren't judging your parental skills; they're empathizing as they remember their own embarrassing family moments."

—BILL DODDS
From "I Coulda Died…"

"My boys will always imagine; I'll see to that. Right now, their imagination is one with mine, and mine with theirs. It's good to be a kid. If only more parents thought so."

—RICHARD G. BEEMER
From "A Father's Ode to Play"

"Forget quality time. You can't plan magic moments or bonding or epiphanies in dealing with kids. What matters is quantity time."

—FRED BARNES
From *The New Republic*, July 12, 1993

"Once Dad wanted my brother Harry and me to repair a 16 by 14 foot wall. Years later Dad explained why... 'When a kid grows up,' he said, 'he needs something that looks impossible to do, and then go out and do it. There are always going to be walls in life.' My father helped us get over one wall, so we would never be scared to take the first step and try to do the impossible."

—WILL SMITH
From *Reader's Digest*, June 1993

"You can mold a mannerism, but you must chisel a character."

—AUTHOR UNKNOWN

"Advice is like snow; the softer it falls the longer it dwells upon, and the deeper it sinks into the mind."

—SAMUEL TAYLOR COLERIDGE

"Man is only miserable so far as he thinks himself so."

—AUTHOR UNKNOWN

"The glory of sons is their fathers."

—PROVERBS 17:6

"Communication with children may be simple, but it is not easy. That's why skilled communicators concentrate on mastering the basics: listening, time, affection, respect. Good basics are more than enough for excellent communication."

—DR. RAY GUARENDI
From *Back to the Family*

"I don't think much of a man who is not wiser today than he was yesterday."

—ABRAHAM LINCOLN

"The simplicity of the child and the profundity of the sage must be combined to make a perfect man."

—AUTHOR UNKNOWN
From Croft M. Pentz's *The Complete Book of Zingers*

"Children will not tolerate us getting away with less than we ask of them. If we curse, smoke, lose our temper, put down others, avoid worship services, leave our half-filled glass on the television, walk through the house with muddy shoes, and these are things we won't let them do, we're going to hear about it, even if it's under their breaths, with their backs to us, on the other side of their locked bedroom door."

—DR. RAY GUARENDI
From *Back to the Family*

"He commanded our fathers, that they should teach…their children, that the generation to come might know, even the children yet to be born…[to] put their confidence in God and…keep His commandments."

—PSALM 78:5-7

THE
FRIEND

"I am with you always,
even to the end of the age."

MATTHEW 28:20

You know what I hate more than anything else? *Alone.*

Separation. Isolation. Alone is hell. And I wasn't made for it. Neither were you.

The Creator said it from the get-go: "It is not good for the man to be alone" (Genesis 2:18). And while the obvious and immediate context is marriage, I believe it is a foundational statement of comprehensive principle to be found throughout Scripture from Genesis to Revelation. Together is better. Men were made to connect. You were made as a friend, for a friend.

My favorite words in all the Bible appear in both the Old and New Testaments. And in each case they are spoken in incredibly significant settings by enormously significant Persons. In the Old Testament, they are the first words spoken to a desperate people by a loving God. In the New Testament, they are the last words spoken to a commissioned people by His Son. First and last, they have a way of marking a friendship.

"I will be with you!"

When God, in a moment of overwhelming intimacy, introduced Himself by name to His despairing but chosen people, the Bible captures it in the vocabulary of friendship: "I have come down to deliver...and to bring up.... I WILL BE WITH YOU!" (Exodus 3:8-12). That sealed it. They had a Friend.

And when Jesus had finished His sacrificial work, just before He ascended to "prepare a place" for His people to join Him at the table forever, He commissioned His disciples in the vocabulary of friendship, saying, "I AM WITH YOU ALWAYS, even to the end of the age" (Matthew 28:20).

Those are words of commitment. They are words of promise. And they are words that drive away all fear, over-whelm the heart with love, and fill the heart with courage.

They are God's words. To you. To me. At His heart, the very core of His eternal essence, our God is a Friend. And man, He created you in His image—for friendship.

The most legendary masculine friendship in all history was marked by very similar words. When David wore a bounty on his head, was within an inch of his life, and at his wit's end after having ducked Saul's spear more than once, "then Jonathan said to David, 'Whatever you say, I will do for you' " (1 Samuel 20:4). That giving away of himself to his friend forged a bond so deep that those two friends carried each other for years.

When Jonathan died on the blood-soaked slopes of Mt. Gilboa, David's heart split and his words pierced the air, "Your love to me was more wonderful than the love of women" (2 Samuel 1:26). Those were not twisted, perverted words. No. They were words straight and true, spoken by a warrior, with the stabbing grief only a soldier mourning for a comrade-in-arms could understand. What the son of Jesse expressed without shame in that lament was something that has burned deep in the soul of every man in one way or another for generations beyond memory.

A desire for friendship, man to man. A yearning for friendship so real, so strong, so compelling, it is willing to share everything about itself and make deep and powerful promises. Down deep at the core, every man needs a friend. Down deep at the core, every man needs a brother to lock arms with. Down deep at the core, men need friends who are men.

"A new commandment I give to you, that you love one another, even as I have loved you, that you also love one another. By this all men will know that you are My disciples, if you have love one for another."

—JOHN 13:34-35

"Oil and perfume make the heart glad. So a man's counsel is sweet to his friend."

—PROVERBS 27:9-10

"Affirming words from moms and dads are like light switches. Speak a word of affirmation at the right moment in a child's life and it's like lighting up a whole roomful of possibilities."

—GARY SMALLEY AND JOHN TRENT
From *Leaving the Light On*

"Affection is responsible for nine-tenths of whatever solid and durable happiness there is in our natural lives."

—C.S. LEWIS
From *The Four Loves*

"Conduct yourselves in a manner worthy of the gospel of Christ…standing firm in one spirit, with one mind striving together for the faith of the gospel."

—PHILIPPIANS 1:27

"Accept one another, then, just as Christ accepted you, in order to bring praise to God."

—ROMANS 15:7 (NIV)

"We aren't with each other only when we have an agenda…. We grasp at opportunities to be with each other…. We don't need an agenda. Nothing needs to happen. Being with each other is an end in itself."

—RICHARD HALVERSON, CHAPLAIN OF THE U.S. SENATE
Of his close friendship with Senator Mark Hatfield; from *Bonds of Iron*

"I love my father, yes. But it has taken half a lifetime to explain to myself how that is possible when like nearly everyone else, I barely know the man…."

—CHRISTOPHER ANDERSEN
From *Father, the Figure and the Force*

LETTER OF LOVE

I must surely say to you, Dad, that you always have been and will continue to be (save perhaps the one God gives me to marry one day) my favorite person on the entire earth—the one I most hope to please, the one for whom I have the most respect, admiration, and awe, and the one I most prefer to spend my time and share my thoughts with.... I will always have a healthy fear of temptation...for I could not bear the thought (forever haunting) of your having reason to be less than pleased with me. Perhaps that motivation is less than ideal in terms of the "eyes of the Savior upon us," but I'm convinced that Christ gives us "little helps" to keep us focused on the goal. Thank God He's given you to me.

—KENT WEBER
A letter to his dad

"I knew wherever I was that you thought of me, and if I got in a tight place you would come—if alive."

—WILLIAM TECUMSEH SHERMAN
In a letter to Ulysses S. Grant

"Once we open our world to another man, we learn that we are not alone in our fears, insecurities, uncertainties and desires.… Through friendship with another man, we affirm much of what is good and strong in us as men. Frank and honest exchanges of experiences allow us to gain a fresh and clear perspective on ourselves."

—DR. KEN DRUCK
From *The Secrets Men Keep*

"Be devoted to one another in brotherly love."

—ROMANS 12:10

"The great man never loses his child's heart."

—AUTHOR UNKNOWN

"Two are better than one…for if either of them falls, the one will lift up his [friend]. But woe to the one who falls when there is not another to lift him up…and if one can overpower him who is alone, two can resist him. A cord of three strands is not quickly torn apart."

—ECCLESIASTES 4:9-12

"…I remembered one morning when I was five years old. After a snowstorm, Dad carried me on his shoulders for the mile from our apartment into town. As he marched bravely through the snowdrifts, I put my hands around his head to hold on, inadvertently covering his eyes with my mittens. 'I can't see,' my father said, but he walked on nevertheless, a blind hero making his way with me on his back through a strange, magical landscape of untrodden snow. What I miss most, ironically, is that time long ago when I was a boy trusting his father to carry him blindly through life and to protect him. The security lay in simply knowing he was there."

— HANK WHITTEMORE
From "On the Shoulders of a Hero," *Reader's Digest*, January 1994

"A soul which remains alone…is like a burning coal which is left by itself: it will grow colder rather than hotter."

— JOHN OF THE CROSS
As quoted in *Mentor and Friend*, by Timothy Jones

"Wrinkles should merely indicate where smiles have been."

— MARK TWAIN

"He who takes the child by the hand takes the mother by the hand."

—AUTHOR UNKNOWN

"Friends are an aid to the young, to guard them from error; to the elderly, to attend to their wants and to supplement their failing power of action; to those in the prime of life, to assist them to noble deeds."

—ARISTOTLE

"To preserve a friend three things are necessary: to honor him present, praise him absent, and assist him in his necessities."

—AUTHOR UNKNOWN

"Home is the place where, when you have to go there, they have to take you in."

—ROBERT FROST

"The best mirror is an old friend."

—GEORGE HERBERT

"To be a friend a man should be tolerant; he should have an understanding heart and a forgiving nature, knowing that all men stumble now and then and that he who never made a mistake never accomplished anything."

—WILFERD A. PETERSON

"Good words shall gain you honor in the marketplace; but good deeds shall gain you friends among men."

—LAO-TSE

"What happiness, what confidence, what joy to have a person to whom you dare to speak on terms of equality as to another self…. You can entrust all the secrets of your heart to him and before him you can lay out all your plans…. No bragging is to be feared and no suspicion need be feared."

—AILRED OF RIEVAULX

"There was a man all alone; he had neither son nor brother. There was no end to his toil."

—ECCLESIASTES 4:8 (NIV)

"Good listening does not mean ceasing whatever we're doing to give our little one our full concentration each and every time he makes it obvious that's what he wants. Other demands on our life don't allow that. Good listening is attempting, whenever possible, to keep an ear open to what a child is asking or saying, even if he takes several hundred words to get to the point."

—DR. RAY GUARENDI
From *Back to the Family*

"Play and pray. They are two sides of the fathering coin.... All play and no pray builds a fun relationship, but one without depth and backbone. All pray and no play leads to bitterness and rejection by the child of both God and father."

—PAUL LEWIS
From "Secrets of a Winning Dad," *Charisma*

"As ye know how we exhorted and comforted and charged every one of you, as a father doth his children."

—1 THESSALONIANS 2:11 (KJV)

"God did not create woman from man's head, that he should command her, nor from his feet, that she should be his slave, but rather from his side, that she should be near his heart."

—HEBREW PROVERB
From *Proverbs to Live By*

"I knew I was special to him—that he was pulling for me and praying for me during each of the small crises that came my way. It's what every little girl needs from a father."

—DANAE DOBSON
From *What My Parents Did Right*

"...When I'd finally connect with the ball—oh, man, I knew I deserved the hit. I'd be grinning all the way down the first-base line.

"I'd turn to look at my father on the pitcher's mound. He'd take off his glove and tuck it under his arm, and then clap for me. To my ears, it sounded like a standing ovation at Yankee Stadium."

—BETH MULLALLY
From "A Lesson from the Mound," *Reader's Digest*

Dear Dad,

I've not forgotten your years of sacrifice—though you probably didn't know I was ever aware of them. I remember the second jobs you took for our comfort. I will never forget how weary you looked as you returned home from your teaching job. After a hasty meal, you would leave again, this time for the factory where you would staple together pasteboard boxes long into the night. And I remember how, despite being exhausted from the week's labors, you would help Mom get four rambunctious children ready for church on Sunday mornings.

Dad, there is so much more I want to say, and so much must go unsaid. I just want you to know how important you are to me—and that I love you.

— STEVE BARCLIFT

Excerpt from letter written to the author's father a few months before his father, Joyce Barclift, died in a traffic accident

"As iron sharpens iron, so one man sharpens another."

— PROVERBS 27:17 (NIV)

"A man that hath friends must show himself friendly."

—PROVERBS 18:24 (KJV)

"Fathering takes time, usually a lifetime, to figure out. It seems that we learn what we need just a few years too late. But I can 'be there' for my children. You may not be skilled, or wise, or educated. But you can take the time for your children.... Fathers, like blue jeans, should wear better with time."

—LARRY KISER

"When he was still a great way off, his father saw him and had compassion, and ran and fell on his neck and kissed him...for his son was dead and is alive again, he was lost and is found."

—LUKE 15:20, 24

"Dads who descend to a child's level to provide comfort even for the small hurts give them a picture of a heavenly Father who cares in the same manner."

—KEN CANFIELD
From "Safe in a Father's Love," *Charisma*

"If I am an effective father, it is because I accept and affirm my children for who they are, appreciate them for what they are accomplishing, and cover them with affection because they are mine."

—GORDON MACDONALD
From *The Effective Father*

"Out of quantity time will come the quality that will communicate your acceptance and appreciation of them."

—JOSH MCDOWELL
From *How to Be a Hero to Your Kids*

"A pedestrian is a man whose son is home from college."

—AUTHOR UNKNOWN
From *To Be a Father*

"The most important thing a father can do for his children is to love their mother."

—THEODORE HESBURGH
President of Notre Dame

"Like many native Italians, my parents were very open with their feelings and their love—not only at home, but also in public. Most of my friends would never hug their fathers. I guess they were afraid of not appearing strong and independent. But I hugged and kissed my dad at every opportunity—nothing could have felt more natural."

—LEE IACOCCA
From *Iacocca: An Autobiography*

"Whether you're short or long on money, the more you give of you, the less your kids will care about worldly goods or any lack of. Time is the essence of parenthood."

—DR. RAY GUARENDI
From *Back to the Family*

"Men are never manlier than when they are tender with their children—whether holding a baby in their arms, loving their gradeschooler, or hugging their teenager or adult children."

—KENT HUGHES
From *Disciplines of a Godly Man*

"Families with good stress-coping skills, generally have fathers who are involved and caring…. They're comfortable kissing a child's hurt or throwing an arm around an adolescent son in affection.

"Much has been written recently about the way children react to fathers and mothers, but it's very clear that men who are not actively involved with the children before adolescence reap the results later on in life in the form of resentful or distant grown children, while those who are involved in the nurturing of young children build a warm relationship with them that endures all their lives."

—DOLORES CURRAN
From *Stress and the Healthy Family*

"A wise son brings joy to his father, but a foolish son grief to his mother."

—PROVERBS 10:1 (NIV)

"An anxious heart weighs a man down, but a kind word cheers him up."

—PROVERBS 12:25 (NIV)

"A gentle answer turns away wrath, but a harsh word stirs up anger."

—PROVERBS 15:1 (NIV)

"Words have awesome power to build us up or tear us down emotionally. This is particularly true within the family. Many people can clearly remember words of praise their parents spoke years ago. Others can remember negative, cutting words—with the whole scene etched in extraordinary detail on their minds."

—GARY SMALLEY AND JOHN TRENT
From *Leaving the Light On*

"If a young girl has a warm, loving, and tender relationship with her father, she will not bring into marriage the deeply embedded feelings of alienation that afflict young women without such dads. She will intuitively believe and expect her husband to treat her in a tender way just as her father treated her."

—STEVE FARRAR
From *Point Man*

"Keep your eyes wide open before marriage, half shut afterwards."

— BENJAMIN FRANKLIN

"So ought men to love their wives as their own bodies. He that loveth his body loveth himself. For no man ever yet hated his own flesh; but nourisheth and cherisheth it, even as the Lord the church: For we are members of his body, of his flesh, and of his bones. For this cause shall a man leave his father and mother, and shall be joined unto his wife, and they two shall be one flesh."

— EPHESIANS 5:28-31 (KJV)

"Married life is a marathon, not a sprint. It is not enough to make a great start toward long-term marriage. You will need the determination to keep plugging on, even when every fiber of your body longs to quit."

— DR. JAMES DOBSON
From *Love for a Lifetime*

"Love is the chain whereby to bind a child to his parents."

— ABRAHAM LINCOLN

"A man and woman should choose each other for life for the simple reason that a long life is barely enough time for a man and woman to understand each other, and to understand is to love."

—DR. GEORGE TRUETT

"The young need old men. They need men who are not ashamed of age, not pathetic imitations of themselves…"

—PETER USTINOV

"Many parents don't realize it, but every child has a touch "bank," and to the degree we maintain a healthy balance in that account, we are helping them to resist immoral relationships and a host of other harmful substitutes for the parental tenderness they crave."

—GARY SMALLEY AND JOHN TRENT

"Let the wife make the husband glad to come home, and let him make her sorry to see him leave."

—MARTIN LUTHER

"He is a creature of vision and she is a lover of touch. By a little unselfish forethought, each can learn to excite the other."

—DR. JAMES DOBSON
From *Love for a Lifetime*

"There be three things which are too wonderful for me, yea, four which I know not: The way of an eagle in the air; the way of a serpent upon a rock; the way of a ship in the midst of the sea; and the way of a man with a maid."

—PROVERBS 30:18-19 (KJV)

"Keeping in mind that the person is eternal who sleeps next to you at night and eats across the table from you each day, has a way of changing the way you treat that individual. Honoring, affirming, and cherishing become a greater desire when we know it can become part of a gift package to God in eternity."

—TIM KIMMEL
From *Little House on the Freeway*

"Gerhard Frost once said that the reason mountain climbers are tied together is to keep the sane ones from going home. That's what marriage is. It is two people tied together as they climb the mountain of life. They have to work as a team."

—STEVE FARRAR
From *Point Man*

"One thing I believe now more than ever before, because I've seen the absolute life-saving nature of it: real men need real men. And real men need open men. I wish that there were more openness among men, that we could sense the true tone of a man's heart."

—DAVE SIMMONS

"You husbands...live with your wives in an understanding way, as with a weaker vessel, since she is a woman; and grant her honor as a fellow heir of the grace of life."

—1 PETER 3:7

"It is not good for the man to be alone."

—GENESIS 2:18 (NIV)

A TIME TO TALK

When a friend calls to me from the road
And slows his horse to a meaning walk,
I don't stand still and look around
On all the hills I haven't hoed,
And shout from where I am, What is it?
No, not as there is a time to talk.
I thrust my hoe in the mellow ground,
Blade-end up and five feet tall,
And plod: I go up to the stone wall
For a friendly visit.

—ROBERT FROST

"Rejoice in the wife of your youth."

—PROVERBS 5:18 (NIV)

"The greatest honor we can give Almighty God is to live gladly because of the knowledge of His love."

—JULIAN OF NORWICH

"Happy is he that is happy in his children."

—THOMAS FULLER

"If you want your children to turn out well, spend twice as much time with them and half as much money."

—AUTHOR UNKNOWN

From Croft M. Pentz's *The Complete Book of Zingers*

THE BUNDLE OF STICKS

A certain man had several sons who were always quarreling with one another, and, try as he might, he could not get them to live together in harmony. So he determined to convince them of their folly by the following means. Bidding them fetch a bundle of sticks, he invited each in turn to break it across his knee. All tried and all failed: and then he undid the bundle, and handed them the sticks one by one, when they had no difficulty at all in breaking them. "There, my boys," said he, "united you will be more than a match for your enemies: but if you quarrel and separate, your weakness will put you at the mercy of those who attack you."…Union is strength.

—AESOP

THE BOY WE WANT

A boy that is truthful and honest
And faithful and willing to work;
But we have not a place that we care to disgrace
With a boy that is ready to shirk.
Wanted—a boy you can tie to,
A boy that is trusty and true,
A boy that is good to old people,
And kind to the little ones too.
A boy that is nice to the home folks,
And pleasant to sister and brother,
A boy who will try when things go awry
To be helpful to father and mother.
These are the boys we depend on—
Our hope for the future, and then
Grave problems of state and the world's work await
Such boys when they grow to be men.

—AUTHOR UNKNOWN

"Reprove a friend in secret, but praise him before others."

—LEONARDO DA VINCI

"Happy the generation where the great listen to the small, for it follows that in such a generation the small will listen to the great."

—HEBREW PROVERB
From *Proverbs to Live By*

"Man strives for glory, honor, fame, that all the world may know his name. He amasses wealth by brain and hand and becomes a power in the land. But when he nears the end of life and looks back o'er the years of strife, he finds that happiness depends on none of these, but love of friends."

—AUTHOR UNKNOWN

"Kindness is a language the deaf can hear and the dumb can understand."

—SENECA

"Better is open rebuke than hidden love. Wounds from a friend can be trusted…"

—PROVERBS 27:5-6 (NIV)

LETTER TO HOME

The following letter was written by a son,
away at college at the time, to his father and two brothers.

Dear Dad, Kent, and Blake,

I'm sitting in my room and have been thinking about my family. We possess a well-kept secret, and I thank you, Dad, for letting us boys in on that secret. I cannot imagine how you instilled in me so much love for my family. I can't express how much I love you, Kent and Blake. I could never have guessed that a person could love another so much. My brothers, I love you. I would fight any giant for you. And, Dad, you are the one with the dedication and commitment that made it all happen—the strength to press on through all the not-so-fun times. Dad, I don't think anybody loves his father as much as I love you.

There could not have been any better living example of the love my Father in heaven has for me than your love, Dad. It is so easy for us, your sons, to understand and experience a true, deep, and intimate relationship with our Father in heaven because of your never-ending, unconditional love.

We have to be the most blessed family around. I love all you guys. I was just sitting here in my room and thinking and praying. I am so lucky. There is no doubt, my brothers, that you will have an incredible impact on this world. I pray for you guys and myself, that He would protect us while we are young. I hope that the Word of God would be on our hearts at all times.... Well, I guess that is enough said. I love you guys and was thinking about you all tonight, and feeling appreciative. I hope everyone has a great day!

—RYAN WEBER

"But the payoff comes when a father and son can move together into an adult relationship. The competition has dissolved forever, and what remains is delicious friendship."

—GORDON DALBEY
From *A Man & His Loves*

"A friend loves at all times, and a brother is born for adversity."

—PROVERBS 17:17 (NIV)

"One day, as we were walking through the only mall in our hometown, I suddenly felt the leather of his letterman's jacket as he put his arm around me. Oh, my. My teenage son with his arm around me in public. 'Dad, I just want you to know that I love you, that I am so proud to have you as my dad.' Everything I had given up ten years earlier could never have meant as much as the sound of those words."

—CHUCK MILLER
From "What's Dad Doing Home So Much?"

"No one is ever stronger and stands higher than when he forgives."

—AUTHOR UNKNOWN
From Croft M. Pentz's *The Complete Book of Zingers*

"Children not only need a father, they long for one, irrationally, with all the undiluted strength of a child's hopeful heart."

—MAGGIE GALLAGHER
From "Points to Ponder," *Reader's Digest*, June 1978

"I'm the luckiest dad in the world to have you for a son."

—TERRY BOATMAN
From *Parents* magazine

"A man never discloses his own character so clearly as when he describes another's."

—JEAN PAUL RICHTER

"...My thoughts drifted back to my father and how much I, when I was a boy, wished I could have known him, not as a man, but when he was a boy. I wished that I could have grown up with him, that he could have been my best friend, that we could have sung the national anthem together, and could have gone to games. My father and I would walk arm in arm, a fantasy so intense that I would sometimes see him before me, imagine him there, talk to him."

—GERAL EARLY
From "An Anthem for my Father" in *Daughters: On Family and Fatherhood*

"Anger is a wind that blows out the mind."

—ROBERT INGERSAL

"A man must at times be hard as nails: willing to face up to the truth about himself and about the woman he loves, refusing to compromise even when he is wrong. But he must also be tender. No weapon will breach the armor of a woman's resentment like tenderness.

"You may not understand her. You may find her unreasonable and illogical and unreachable by any means other than honest tenderness. If she can believe, even for a second or two, that you really want to understand her, that you are earnestly trying to see things from her point of view, she will budge. I know. I'm a woman, and I appear unbudgeable to some, but I also know what a man's arms around me will do to my defenses."

—ELISABETH ELLIOT
From *Mark of a Man*

"And He died for all, that those who live should no longer live for themselves but for Him who died and rose again on their behalf."

—2 CORINTHIANS 5:15

"He who walks with the wise grows wise, but a companion of fools suffers harm."

—PROVERBS 13:20 (NIV)

"I came to realize after several disastrous affairs that all the men I fall in love with are just like my dad. Physically, they are tall, athletic, handsome. Emotionally, they are close-mouthed, unfeeling, and *cold.*"

—LINDA, AGE 32
From *Father, the Figure and the Force*

"Today, as a grandfather of six, it is increasingly apparent that my most treasured possessions, next to life in Christ, are the members of my family.... Someday when all is gone, when I can no longer see or hear or talk—indeed when I may no longer know their names—the faces of my loved ones will be on my soul."

—KENT HUGHES
From *Disciplines of a Godly Man*

"The great man is he who does not lose his child's heart."

—MENCIUS, 371-288 B.C.

"Whether playing a game of catch or lending a sympathetic ear, dads can make a big difference. Indeed, the more fathers invest in their families, the better off they and their children will be later in life."

— MARJORY ROBERTS
From *The Benefits of Fatherhood*

"Effective fathers know not only the developmental needs of their children at various stages of their growth, but they also know the specific, unique qualities of each son or daughter. They have taken the time and effort to discover and remember the details of each child's world: their gifts, their fears and disappointments, their dreams, the names and personalities of their friends, as well as knowing the things that upset, embarrass, motivate, and encourage each child."

— KEN CANFIELD
From "The Seven Secrets of Effective Fatherhood"

"Courage is what it takes to stand up and speak; courage is also what it takes to sit down and listen."

— AUTHOR UNKNOWN

"Laugh a lot with your kids. Find the humor in their behavior. They can be absolute characters sometimes. Learn to laugh at yourself. Sometimes we grownups are bigger characters than the kids."

—DR. RAY GUARENDI
From *Back to the Family*

"Thanks for being my father." He was quiet on his end.
My mother was too.
The static of the long-distance line filled the void.
"I wish I'd been better," he said, his voice subdued.
"You were just fine," I said.
"A guy couldn't have had a better father."
"Good of you to say, but not true. I wish it were," he said with regret in his voice. "I'll hang up now. Don't want to run up your bill." His voice was shaking.
…After I hung up, I looked at the photograph of Father and me together in Maine. I wiped my eyes and smiled at the picture and blew my nose loudly.

—GEORGE EYRE MASTERS
From "Thanks for Being My Father," in *Reader's Digest*

"…All too soon it is dark. And all too soon fathers must stop playing catch with sons."

—BOB MORRIS
From "An Enduring Game of Catch," *Reader's Digest*

"One hundred years from now, it will not matter what kind of car I drove, what kind of house I lived in, how much money I had, nor what my clothes looked like. But the world may be a little better, the universe a little brighter, because I was important to a child."

—AUTHOR UNKNOWN

"Real listening means taking some radical steps. Like putting the newspaper down. Or turning off the tube (horrors!). It means leaning forward a little. If the speaker is little, it may mean getting down on your knees. Just imagine yourself five-foot-five, living in a world populated by nine-foot giants. It gets tiresome craning your neck all the time!"

—GARY SMALLEY AND JOHN TRENT

"You can't beat love. You have to have those hugs, those kisses, yet still know how to say, 'You've done wrong.' "

—BILL COSBY
Quoted in *Redbook*

John,

The things that I am going to say in this letter are about twenty years and a whole lifetime late, but maybe that won't matter once they've been said.

We trusted each other, implicitly. We depended on each other. We supported each other. We shared a whole lot in the time that we knew each other: pain, hunger, sickness, triumph, laughter, and more than a little excitement. We even shared a lover, Death. Both of us wooed [her], but you won her. What a deal for you. You know, I've never forgiven you for leaving me alone. I've been alone and lonely ever since.

I never thanked you for the times that you saved my life. Any more than you thanked me for the times that I saved yours. I kind of thought that it was understood, and didn't matter.... It does seem to mean something now. It's important. Thanks....

A lot of the guys who were there say they feel like they lost something in [that] country: I know what I lost. I've always said that when you died, it was like killing the other half of myself. Maybe that's not necessarily true. What I did lose was youth...all of the idealism, trust, self-confidence, and personal power that we had, either inside or drilled into us. I'm scared, now, most of the time, and I hurt a lot.

What happened to us has cost me a life as much as it cost you yours....

I never got to say good-bye. So I've come to this monument to have a little memorial service and to say good-bye and to let you go. I'll never forget you, don't worry about that.

—AUTHOR UNKNOWN
From a letter left at the Vietnam Memorial Wall

"Is any pleasure on earth as great as a circle of Christian friends by a fire?"

—C.S. LEWIS
From *Letters of C.S. Lewis*